Fetch This Book
Train Your Dog to Do Almost Anything

OUR BEST FRIENDS

The Beagle

The Boxer

The Bulldog

Caring for Your Mutt

The Dachshund

Ferrets

Fetch this Book

Gerbils

The German Shepherd

The Golden Retriever

Guinea Pigs

Hamsters

The Labrador Retriever

Lizards

The Miniature Schnauzer

Mixed Breed Cats

The Poodle

The Pug

Rabbits

The Rottweiler

The Shih Tzu

Snakes

Turtles

The Yorkshire Terrier

OUR BEST FRIENDS

Fetch This Book
Train Your Dog to Do Almost Anything

Elaine Waldorf Gewirtz

ELDORADO INK

Produced by OTTN Publishing, Stockton, New Jersey

Eldorado Ink
PO Box 100097
Pittsburgh, PA 15233
www.eldoradoink.com

CPSIA compliance information: Batch#101909-4. For further information, contact
Eldorado Ink at info@eldoradoink.com.

First printing

1 3 5 7 9 8 6 4 2

Library of Congress Cataloging-in-Publication Data

  Gewirtz, Elaine Waldorf.
   Fetch this book : train your dog to do almost anything / Elaine Waldorf Gewirtz.
     p. cm. — (Our best friends)
   Includes bibliographical references and index.
   ISBN 978-1-932904-60-4
   1. Dogs—Training. I. Title.
   SF431.G49 2010
   636.7'0887—dc22

                  2009041441

**For information about custom editions, special sales, or premiums,
please contact our special sales department at info@eldoradoink.com.**

TABLE OF CONTENTS

Introduction

The mutually beneficial relationship between humans and animals began long before the dawn of recorded history. Archaeologists believe that humans began to capture and tame wild goats, sheep, and pigs more than 9,000 years ago. These animals were then bred for specific purposes, such as providing humans with a reliable source of food or providing furs and hides that could be used for clothing or the construction of dwellings.

Other animals had been sought for companionship and assistance even earlier. The dog, believed to be the first animal domesticated, began living and working with Stone Age humans in Europe more than 14,000 years ago. Some archaeologists believe that wild dogs and humans were drawn together because both hunted the same prey. By taming and training dogs, humans became more effective hunters. Dogs, meanwhile, enjoyed the social contact with humans and benefited from greater access to food and warm shelter. Dogs soon became beloved pets as well as trusted workers. This can be seen from the many artifacts depicting dogs that have been found at ancient sites in Asia, Europe, North America, and the Middle East.

The earliest domestic cats appeared in the Middle East about 5,000 years ago. Small wild cats were probably first attracted to human settlements because plenty of rodents could be found wherever harvested grain was stored. Cats played a useful role in hunting and killing these pests, and it is likely that grateful humans rewarded them for this assistance. Over time, these small cats gave up some of their aggressive wild behaviors and began living among humans. Cats eventually became so popular in ancient Egypt that they were believed to possess magical powers. Cat statues were placed outside homes to ward off evil spirits, and mummified cats were included in royal tombs to accompany their owners into the afterlife.

Today, few people believe that cats have supernatural powers, but most pet owners feel a magical bond with their pets, whether they are dogs, cats, hamsters, rabbits, horses, or parrots. The lives of pets and their people become inextricably intertwined, providing strong emotional and physical rewards for both humans and animals. People of all ages can benefit from the loving companionship of a pet. Not surprisingly, then, pet ownership is widespread. Recent statistics indicate that about 60 percent of all households in the United States and Canada have at least one pet, while the figure is close to 50 percent of households in the United Kingdom. For millions of people, therefore, pets truly have become their "best friends."

Finding the best animal friend can be a challenge, however. Not only are there many types of domesticated pets, but each has specific needs, characteristics, and personality traits. Even within a category of pets, such as dogs, different breeds will flourish in different surroundings and with different treatment. For example, a German Shepherd may not be the right pet for a person living in a cramped urban apartment; that person might be better off caring for a smaller dog like a Toy Poodle or Shih Tzu, or perhaps a cat. On the other hand, an active person who loves the outdoors may prefer the companion-ship of a Labrador Retriever to that of a small dog or a passive indoor pet like a goldfish or hamster.

The joys of pet ownership come with certain responsibilities. Bringing a pet into your home and your neighborhood obligates you to care for and train the pet properly. For example, a dog must be housebroken, taught to obey your commands, and trained to behave appropriately when he encounters other people or animals. Owners must also be mindful of their pet's particular nutritional and medical needs.

The purpose of the OUR BEST FRIENDS series is to provide a helpful and comprehensive introduction to pet ownership. Each book contains the basic information a prospective pet owner needs in order to choose the right pet for his or her situation and to care for that pet throughout the pet's lifetime. Training, socialization, proper nutrition, potential medical issues, and the legal responsibilities of pet ownership are thoroughly explained and discussed, and an abundance of expert tips and suggestions are offered. Whether it is a hamster, corn snake, guinea pig, or Labrador Retriever, the books in the OUR BEST FRIENDS series provide everything the reader needs to know about how to have a happy, well-adjusted, and well-behaved pet.

Training a dog to obey your commands will make him a happier pet, and will allow you to feel more comfortable taking him out in public.

CHAPTER ONE

Why Training Is Good

Congratulations! You've acquired a four-footed bundle of fluff. Now he's yours for life.

For the first few days, your dog was a model pup. Lately, though, he seems to prefer munching on the chair leg to eating all of his breakfast. Whenever the doorbell rings, he flies into a frenzy or leaves a puddle on the carpet. And when he's outside, he insists on digging up the rose bushes in the yard.

What to do? Train your dog. Teach him the difference between behaving badly and minding his p's and q's. As his best friend, it's your job to establish the rules. Work with him to transform his unacceptable behavior into exemplary conduct.

Make him the kind of dog who brings a little bit of joy to every day.

If you're concerned that formal lessons will ruin your dog's fun-loving, free spirit, guess again. You don't have to be a marine drill sergeant to train your dog. In fact, good training requires a trusting relationship, and positive methods work best. If you learn to understand your dog's nonverbal communication and reward his good behavior, he'll naturally want to obey your rules.

The right training boosts your dog's self-confidence. It gives him the skills to be a good canine citizen and to work out problems on his own. A dog that is trained to respond to your instructions will be a lot more fun as a companion. Besides, everything you do with him—from trimming his toenails and convincing him to like his crate to going potty outside and behaving at the veterinarian's office—involves training.

When it comes to training, you're actually just taking over where your dog's mother and siblings left off. From the moment your pup opened his eyes, his mother and his brothers and sisters started teaching him how to behave. With a shake and a nip they let him know when he played too rough. They edged him off the food tray if he dawdled at chowtime. Now, you are your dog's coach. You're teaching him the ways of the world.

BUILDING A BOND

During training you may feel ecstatic when your dog understands what you're trying to teach him. On the other hand, you may feel frustration when he doesn't get it. This is a normal part of the training process. Through it all you'll need lots of patience.

Despite what many people think, no one knows all the tricks the first, second, or even third time they train a dog. Some people have been lucky enough to grow up with dogs. Thus they've had a chance to observe, from an early age, how to use positive training methods. But

even if you didn't have this advantage, it's never too late to learn how to train a dog. Good trainers continually develop and refine their canine knowledge and skills. So particularly if you're a novice trainer, be patient with your dog and yourself. Remember that you're both learning from the process.

Through training you'll build a bond with your new four-footed friend that will last a lifetime. What does bonding with your dog mean? It means you and your dog will share a dynamic and rewarding relationship. He'll give you unconditional love no matter what you look like, what kind of car you drive, or how much money you make. On your part, you've made a choice to add your canine companion to your life, and you'll put up

FAST FACT

You'll get much better results from training sessions if you're relaxed, rested, and focused. As soon as you begin feeling impatient, frustrated, or angry at your dog, stop the training session. Also, don't try to multitask when training your dog. Turn off the TV and your cell phone, and make sure any other pets are in a different room.

with his shedding, muddy feet, drool, and dog breath.

When your dog has a strong bond with you, he listens to your instructions because this is the normal routine. When the two of you are outside, he doesn't think of wandering off, even when there's an interesting distraction to check out, such as another dog or some sweet-smelling flowers down the street. Inside your home, you can trust him to respect your belongings and to greet your guests warmly but not aggressively.

Having a strong bond with your dog has other advantages. When you have a good relationship with your dog, taking him for a car ride—or even on a family vacation—is a breeze. He's well mannered, pays attention to the world around him, and is a joyous companion. He accepts a toenail trim, loves a sudsy bath, and respects the boundaries of a leash while on a walk.

Creating a strong bond with your dog won't give you a perfect pooch. But it will go a long way toward ensuring that you have an excellent

A well-trained dog is a joy to be around.

companion. And remember that it's never too late to establish a relationship with a dog, no matter how old he is. All it takes is dedication, patience, and confidence that you can succeed.

MEETING THE WORLD

One of the best ways to strengthen your relationship with a puppy is to introduce him to new sights, sounds, and experiences. This includes introducing him to other dogs and new people. You and your dog will share the fun. Plus, your dog will receive important socialization, part of a life-long desensitization process that will help him stay calm and relaxed in new situations.

Before venturing out, ask your veterinarian to give your puppy a clean bill of health. Ideally, the time to begin socializing a puppy is between the ages of 8 and 18 weeks, because dogs at this age are more open to new experiences. After this time, distrust of anything unfamiliar begins to set in, and it takes longer for a dog to recognize that the world around him is not a scary place.

But even if you've adopted an older dog, it's not too late to introduce him to the outside world. Your

NIGHTTIME TRAINING

Begin bonding with your dog the first night you bring him home. For a puppy, a sleepover in his new digs can be scary. He's away from his mother and siblings for the first time, and all of the sights, sounds, and smells are different. Even an older dog may feel insecure in an unfamiliar place. If you leave your new dog alone in another room on his first night at your home, he may feel frightened and howl. To reassure him, let him sleep in your bedroom on his first night. Put him next to your bed, either in a crate or on a blanket with his leash looped around the leg of the bed frame.

An hour before you're ready for bed, play with your dog to tire him out a bit. Then take him outside to use the potty. Bring him indoors, give him a hug, and tell him "good night" before putting him in his crate or on his blanket. Turn out the light. He may whimper a little at first, but you should resist the urge to take him out of his crate or pick him up. Instead, put your fingers through the crate openings or near his blanket and speak kind words to him. This way he'll know you're nearby.

adopted dog may cower or shake around people, or he may act aggressively by lunging or barking excessively. Many people assume a dog that displays these behaviors was once abused, but that isn't necessarily the case. In fact, these behaviors usually occur because the dog was never socialized properly. Because he never learned how to act around people, around other dogs, or outside the home in general, the dog lacks confidence. You can fix that, but you'll want to proceed slowly. At first, take your dog out on the street only for a few minutes per day. Increase the time gradually as he becomes more comfortable and confident.

Whenever you do take your pooch outside for socialization—whether he's a puppy or an adopted adult dog—make sure he's on his leash. Also, pack along some doggy treats. Go to different neighborhoods and visit a variety of places, from the carwash and cleaners to outdoor cafés, nurseries, and storefronts. Don't shy away from blaring distractions such as cars honking, children skateboarding, and construction crews hammering and drilling.

Your dog may be frightened at first. But you should ignore any undesirable reactions that he shows, such as jumping, pulling at the leash, barking, or cowering. Whatever you do, don't coddle him or say reassuringly, "Don't worry, boy, it's OK." This will just reinforce the behavior you're trying to change. Instead, praise him and give him a treat as soon as the undesirable behavior stops. Do the same whenever he takes a distraction in stride by sitting politely, walking calmly, or sniffing quietly. Eventually he'll realize that staying calm, relaxed, and well behaved earns him major brownie points.

How long should you continue socializing your dog? This depends on your dog's breed, personality, and comfort level. All dogs like to get out of the house and see new sights, but some dogs need more social experience than others. In general, the more places your dog can tag along with you, the sooner he'll learn to behave appropriately.

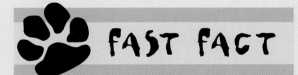

FAST FACT

When a dog receives attention for an undesired behavior—even if the attention is negative—the behavior is reinforced. Never punish your dog by hitting or yelling at him.

THE CENTER FOR THE HUMAN-ANIMAL BOND

In 1982 the Purdue University School of Veterinary Medicine established the Center for the Human-Animal Bond. The center seeks to expand knowledge of the interrelationships between people, animals, and the environment. It also promotes animal welfare.

Researchers associated with the Center for the Human-Animal Bond have examined how people in nursing homes, hospitals, hospices, and prisons can benefit from visits from animals. Studies have shown that when people are around animals, they experience decreased blood pressure, reduced anxiety, and an overall feeling of well-being. Children learn to be more sensitive and nurturing and may grow up to be better parents to their own children because they have learned how to care for dogs.

HOUSE RULES

You don't need to wait until your dog is comfortable outside before beginning his indoor lessons. Socialization and indoor training should be taught together. As your dog learns what you expect of him outdoors, he'll more easily accept your rules inside the house, where there are fewer distractions.

To reinforce training, it helps if the whole family agrees to follow the same lesson plans. Establish some goals and guidelines that everyone will abide by and enforce. These should include:

- Teaching the dog to sit before receiving his meal. This prevents the dog from knocking the bowl out of your hand and helps him understand that you are in charge of his food.

- Insisting that your dog sits and stays before you open any door. This prevents him from slamming into you or escaping from the house and running into the street. Children should be taught never to open the door without an adult present to watch the dog.

- Instructing the dog to follow you through open doorways. This establishes that you are in charge.

- Teaching your dog that you decide where in the house he's allowed to wander. If you don't

Your dog should be trained to sit and stay before you open a door.

want him in your bedroom, for example, never permit him there. If you don't want him on your couch, recliner, or other chairs, never allow him to sit or lie down on the furniture. Be sure your dog has a dog bed, crate, or other area of his own, however. Teach him that you decide when he's allowed out of his area.

- Choosing when you will give your dog attention, instead of letting him annoy you by licking or pawing at you to pet him. Some dogs are overly needy and want constant feedback from their owners. To change this behavior, completely ignore your dog when he badgers you. Telling him "no" or yelling at him will only reinforce his irritating behavior.

- Ignoring begging behavior. Never feed the dog from the table. If you want to give your dog healthy tidbits, place them in his food bowl for a later meal. Once you hand out treats directly from the table, he'll beg (and bug you!) for the rest of his life.

- Repeating a command only once. This teaches your dog to pay attention to what you say the first time. Say his name first and then give a one-word command, such as "Joey, sit."

- Expecting your dog to follow your command. If you give a command to your dog, make sure that he does what you ask him to do. If you tell your dog to sit or to stay, he should remain in those positions until you tell him that it's OK to move. If he moves prematurely, physically help him return to the right position.

- Controlling access to food. Your dog shouldn't be helping himself to the food bag or nibbling at his meals throughout the day.

With everyone in the household sharing in the dog's care and training, and with consistent enforcement of the rules, your dog will learn quickly.

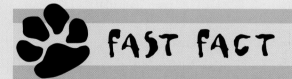

FAST FACT

You should never call your dog to come to you so you can reprimand him. He'll remember this and ignore you the next time you call him.

If you don't want your dog begging at the table, don't feed him scraps from the table. Doing this even once gives your canine pal a reason to keep coming back.

TRAINING BASICS

To facilitate your dog's training, set goals for what you want to teach him, and plan out each session. Keep in mind that dogs learn fastest through short, frequent sessions. Long, sporadic training sessions tend to tire them out and confuse them. In addition to keeping practice sessions short, be generous with the rewards. Reinforce the right behaviors with food treats that really motivate your dog. Above all, stay positive.

CHAPTER TWO

What Your Dog Thinks About Training

You say to your dog, "Joey, come!" He runs the other way and looks out the window. What's going on? Has your command been lost in translation? Is your dog trying to tell you something? Many a frustrated dog owner has wished for a canine language translator or a Webster's "dogtionary."

In addition to their bark, dogs communicate with one another through a whole set of nonverbal signals. These include posture, facial expression, and movements.

Consider the following example. Two dogs encounter each other in a park. One stands tall, with his ears up and forward, his tail back, and

Dogs indicate dominance or submission through their body language.

his eyes maintaining a fixed gaze. The other rolls on the ground, upside down. The dogs are speaking volumes to each other. But the meaning might be lost on a human observer who is unfamiliar with doggy lingo. Such a person might conclude that the dog rolling on the ground wants to play, while the standing dog isn't interested. In fact, the rolling dog is acknowledging his submissiveness to the standing dog, whose posture communicates his dominant status.

If you're a novice dog owner, the world of canine communication may seem very complex. How will you ever learn what your pup is trying to tell you? Don't despair. Your dog is a great communicator. In time, you'll be able to figure out what he's feeling and thinking by closely observing his body language.

If his ears are up, his eyes are bright and shining, and his tail is wagging, your dog is signaling to you that he is happy. Ears back, curled

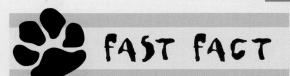

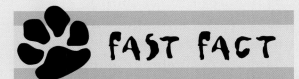

A dog's physical limitations may affect training. For example, a heavy dog may be reluctant to sit up or jump, as these actions may put stress on his joints and cause pain.

lips, and tail down spells anger, fear, or stress. Panting, yawning, or drooling can be a sign of stress or fear in an unfamiliar situation or location. Crouching down on all fours is an invitation to play with you, while sniffing the ground or looking away translate to "Bug off, I don't want to be bothered."

It takes two to communicate, so your dog needs to understand you as well. With time he will be able to comprehend what a few of your words mean, read hand signals, and interpret your body language. Raising your voice and keeping the pitch low will get his attention. A catch in your breath signals to your dog that you are feeling nervous, upset, or happy.

Your dog behaves in response to the signals you send, so controlling your demeanor and projecting calmness will go a long way toward easing your dog's fear or nervousness. When you are unsure or anxious, your dog

In general, females of a given breed are easier to train than males of the same breed. There are always exceptions, however.

will pick up on these feelings, and he will become even more nervous. Dog trainers often say that their own emotions go right down the leash to the dog.

EVALUATE PERSONALITY

Like people, all dogs—regardless of breed—are individuals. They have unique personalities. Because of this, the best approach to training one dog might not be the best approach to training another. As you train your pup, you should be guided by some

Dog personalities are as varied as those of their owners. Understanding your dog's temperament and personality traits will enable you to find the most effective training techniques.

basic do's and don'ts. But you should also be aware that you might have to try a few different approaches before achieving success.

A good first step is to assess your pup's temperament. Is your dog confident, pushy, dominant, funny, fearful, bold, or aggressive? It helps to size him up so you can tailor your training style to match your dog's needs. If you are too easygoing with a strong, bold dog, he may push the limits of the training. On the other hand, using strong, overbearing training techniques with a shy, nervous dog will probably just scare him more.

Easygoing dogs, like easygoing people, go with the flow. Calm and mellow, they seem to take everything in stride. While this is a good thing, an easygoing pup might not always be the most motivated. Often the best approach to training this type of dog is to be firm and in control.

High-strung dogs or dogs with in-your-face personalities present special challenges. Training dogs like this requires a lot of control; a strong, stable voice; good problem-solving skills; and special attention.

Before beginning training, take the time to assess all aspects of your dog's personality. What is his attention span? How does he respond to distractions? What are his favorite types of toys? Is he relentless until he gets what he wants, or does he give up easily? Understanding his learning style will help you establish your training goals.

JUDGING ENERGY LEVEL

A good training program takes into consideration your pup's energy level. Does your dog love to sunbathe in the yard all day, or does he live for chasing squirrels? If you have an active, high-energy dog, shape your training to take advantage of his enthusiasm. Short, to-the-point training sessions with simple goals work well.

Dogs that are more content with quieter activities will need more motivation to get up and moving. Keep training sessions short because these dogs figure things out quickly and don't feel the need to repeat drills. Food treats may be a good source of motivation, but only if your dog hasn't just eaten.

Many medium-energy dogs respond well to repeated training

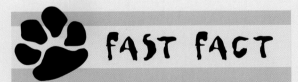

FAST FACT

The critical socialization stage for puppies is 8 to 16 weeks of age. During this time puppies can learn to accept and be comfortable with a variety of sights, sounds, people, and places.

sessions and a variety of training methods. This is because these dogs are often eager to please you.

GETTING HELP

After you're armed with some knowledge about your dog's personality, you should be ready to begin applying this knowledge to his training. However, if you've never trained a puppy before, the task may seem overwhelming. Or, perhaps you've adopted a dog that needs more training than you feel you can provide on your own. In these circumstances you may want to consider hiring a private trainer or signing up to attend obedience classes with your dog.

While a private trainer can train your dog quickly, this is often a very expensive way to get the job done. Among the benefits to having a private trainer are receiving one-on-one attention for solving problems and not having to leave your own home.

To locate a professional trainer, ask your veterinarian, breeder, or other dog owners for referrals. You can also contact the Association of Pet Dog Trainers (www.apdt.com), the National Association of Dog Obedience Instructors (www.nadoi.org), or the International Association of Canine Professionals (www.dogpro.org). Interview trainers before committing. Ask whether

Hiring a private trainer has certain advantages, particularly if you are a novice dog owner. A professional will not only train your dog, she'll also teach you how to be a more effective canine leader.

they've had experience with your dog's breed or whether they've dealt with any problems you may be experiencing with your dog.

Attending obedience classes with your dog provides support in a group setting. Group classes provide a perfect socialization opportunity for young puppies that need to meet other dogs and people. Depending on the class size, you might not receive any intensive, one-on-one training, as you would if you hired a private trainer. However, obedience classes are less expensive than private trainers, and some classes offer private sessions by appointment. This may be especially helpful if you are a new dog owner and have a zillion questions to ask.

When taught by an experienced trainer, a good obedience course offers instruction in a safe, supervised environment. In addition to the socialization benefits for dogs, the group setting allows owners to learn from one another, to observe the step-by-step progression of training exercises, and to watch a veteran trainer in action. This will yield valuable insights and tips you can use with your own dog. However, for dogs with severe behavior problems such as aggression toward people or other animals, phobias, or separation anxiety, you may need more private attention than a group class can offer.

To locate a good class or training school in your area, ask your veterinarian, breeder, or other dog owners for recommendations. Your kennel club may also sponsor classes. Look for schools that limit class size to one instructor or assistant for every six students. It helps if there are assistants or volunteers on site to answer questions, manage the class, or give you private attention if necessary. It helps, too, if the instructor distributes written handouts or homework sheets so you can refresh your memory at home and share the lessons with other family members.

PUPPY KINDERGARTEN

To give your puppy a great first training experience, consider enrolling him in a puppy kindergarten class, also known as puppy preschool. These classes accept puppies up to four months of age. A typical puppy kindergarten lasts six weeks, meeting once a week for about an hour.

Puppy kindergarten is less structured than obedience class. In puppy kindergarten, you and your pup interact with other owners and their pups in a relaxed social environment. An instructor explains puppy behavior, gives suggestions on housetraining and other common training issues, and leads the group through activities, learning exercises, and guided play.

SAFE TRAINING SURFACES

During training your dog's safety should always come first. Never train in hot or very cold weather, and be sure to feel the ground where your dog is standing. Asphalt, blacktop, and concrete can heat up quickly and burn the pads of a dog's feet. It's no wonder that a dog may refuse to sit or lie down on these surfaces in extreme weather. Practice instead on a cool, comfortable surface such as grass, dirt, or carpeting. Also avoid slick surfaces that may cause your dog to slip and fall.

PURE OR MIXED BREED?

When choosing a dog, think about how much time you'll be able to devote to training. In addition to their distinctive physical characteristics, different breeds have different personality traits. Some breeds require more training than others.

For breed information, consult the American Kennel Club's Web site. Talk to breeders and ask about breed traits. Dogs that were originally bred to perform jobs alongside their owners, such as German Shepherds and Border Collies, are more willing to please than breeds whose roots began more independently. Other breeds that are particularly devoted to their owners include Labrador Retrievers, Golden Retrievers, Shetland Sheepdogs, Cavalier King Charles Spaniels, French Bulldogs, Cocker Spaniels, Pugs, and Poodles.

Even if you don't plan to get a purebred, researching breed types can pay dividends. You'll find it easier to choose a mixed-breed dog at a shelter if you know you want "something like a Labrador" or "a terrier type."

Puppy kindergarten can be great fun for owners and their cuddly companions alike. But it should be more than an extended romp. A good puppy kindergarten will not only help you bond with your puppy, but also provide some solid early training for your canine companion. Your puppy can learn how to get along with other pooches and people. Since many puppy kindergartens allow the whole family to attend, your puppy might have a chance to learn how to act around children even if you don't have any kids yourself. Best of all, your puppy can receive positive reinforcement in a fun, non-stressful environment. There's no yelling, leash corrections, or withholding attention.

To locate a puppy kindergarten class, contact the American Kennel Club (www.akc.com) or your local kennel club, veterinarian, or breeder. Before committing to a six-week session with your puppy, ask if you can observe a class. The socialization should be positive, and you should

FAST FACT

Increase the amount of exercise your dog receives every day and he'll pay more attention during training.

Completing puppy kindergarten can be a fun milestone for you to share. Like this family, you can take "graduation" portraits to remember the day.

feel comfortable with the instructor's methods and the way the class is organized.

PROVIDING A FOUNDATION

With good early training, your dog will learn lessons that benefit him throughout his lifetime. Yet it is not the case, as some owners mistakenly believe, that a dog's need to learn ends once puppy kindergarten or other early training has been completed. All dogs, no matter what the breed, are intelligent creatures that need regular mental stimulation—just as they need regular exercise—to have a good quality of life. You can keep your dog's mind sharp through-

out his life by continually giving him new things to think about and offering him new challenges.

Good early training is so important because it greatly facilitates later learning. It lays a solid foundation. Yes, you can teach a dog that has missed out on early socialization. But chances are that training him will be a long, difficult slog. It's not that the dog is dumb or stubborn. He just never developed the ability to focus, and he can't grasp the connection between the reward you give him and the change in behavior you want. With such a dog, you will have to be extremely patient.

CHAPTER THREE

Establishing Who's in Charge

You've told your dog to get off the bed about a zillion times. But where do you find him when you return from a trip to the grocery store? On your bed, nestled in the comforter and fast asleep.

If you really want to stop your snuggle bunny from dancing in the sheets—or from any other undesirable behavior—repeat the following: "My dog is not in charge of the household. I am!" Many owners have

Your dog must learn that his place is not on the furniture.

a hard time setting rules for their dogs. They feel badly every time they deny their canine companion something he wants. But dogs are pack animals, and they need a leader to establish the limits.

Remember: in your home you are first in command. You decide where your dog sleeps, when and where he eats, what toys he has, and how he receives attention, playtime, and outings. Your dog should never jump on the bed or couch and growl at you when you tell him to move, pester you unmercifully to pet him, or run through the doorway ahead of you. Ignoring you when you call him? This is totally unacceptable behavior.

But being in charge doesn't mean that you force your dog to submit to your every whim or are harsh with corrections. On the contrary. As a leader you provide a safe, nurturing environment. But you also set the agenda and control the resources. When your dog understands who has the power, he will more readily grasp what's expected of him, especially when you introduce a new training concept.

CONSISTENCY COUNTS

Good dog training is all about maintaining the top position in the household and being consistent

FAST FACT

The best way to teach your dog a new behavior is to break it down into individual steps. Begin with an easy skill and gradually increase the difficulty.

about the rules you set. This means enforcing the same habits 24/7.

Perhaps you don't want your puppy sleeping in your bed when you have to get up for work or school the next morning, but you'd be OK with him sleeping in your bed on weekends. The arrangement sounds workable enough. It isn't. Your pooch will never understand the concept of "sometimes." When you boot him out on Sunday night after welcoming him on Friday and Saturday night, he'll be confused. He won't know what you expect of him. That's why it's important to be consistent.

This isn't to say that you can never change your mind about a

FAST FACT

With dog training, timing is crucial. After your dog performs a desired behavior, reward him instantly. This way he connects the behavior with the reward.

doggy rule. For example, you might always have allowed your dog to sit on the furniture, but after getting an expensive new couch and chairs, you decide that you want him to stay on the floor. Now you'll have to say "no" every time he leaps up on the furniture, redirect him to a place on the floor, put him in a down/stay position, and then tell him he's a good dog. Stick by the new directive and he'll soon figure out that the rules have changed. Later on, after the furniture has gotten a few stains or nicks, you might be tempted to soften up your discipline and let your dog back on the couch. Think twice before doing so, as you will again be causing him confusion.

Consistency in training works with any behavior you want to change, whether it's sitting on the furniture or begging from the table, knocking the food bowl out of your hand, barking, or housetraining. But adhering to the plan you've set for your dog is often a challenge. If you're running late for an appointment or feeling exhausted after a long day at work, for example, you might be inclined to allow an instance of bad doggy behavior to slide. Don't. If you want him to follow your directions, you shouldn't make any exceptions.

USING POSITIVE METHODS

From dog trainers on television to part-time hobbyists who call themselves trainers, everyone seems to have a theory about the best way to train a dog. Good training all boils down to rewarding the behavior you want and ignoring the behavior you don't want.

MANY DOGS, ONE LEADER

With multiple dogs in a house, aggression may develop if there's no clear pack leader. Here's where the owner must step up and assume the top position. When the dogs know who the leader is, the fighting generally stops.

Help the dogs establish their pack order by showing the weaker or younger dogs that the oldest dog is higher in the canine chain of command. Feed, walk, and play with the oldest dog first, and give the oldest dog more attention. If you bring in a puppy or a younger dog, keep to this plan.

Dogs learn acceptable behavior by observing how you react to their actions. If they receive a positive reaction such as verbal praise, a food treat, or a petting after they perform a certain behavior, they'll start repeating that behavior. On the other hand, if you ignore them and don't even make eye contact after they perform a behavior, they'll eventually stop that behavior. Dogs really want to please you so they can earn a reward. The idea is to control your dog's behavior by limiting his access to what he wants.

Never punish a dog by hitting, scolding, or yanking him with a hard leash correction. While this may work in the beginning, it doesn't do the trick in the long term and can even backfire. Your dog may turn to growling or barking at you the next

Food treats, accompanied by praise, are a great way to reinforce desirable behavior. However, don't overdo it, as too many treats can make your canine pal obese. Break treats into several pieces, and make sure to consider them part of your pet's daily caloric intake.

time you come near him because he was hurt. Teach your dog to do what you want by rewarding him.

KIDS AND DOGS

Children and puppies go together like peanut butter and jelly. They're usually inseparable, but parents need to supervise them. During rambunctious play, children can accidentally hurt a little dog, whereas a bigger dog can unintentionally knock down a small tot. Kids must be taught to be careful with their dogs. They should also know that it is never acceptable to tease or torment the dog by grabbing or pulling the tail, ears, or coat.

Puppies love to chew. And before you've fully trained them, they'll chomp down on just about anything—including a child's fingers or hands. When this happens, the child's natural reaction will be to scream and run away. Unfortunately, the puppy will think this is all a game and may chase after the child to bite again. It's easy to see how this situation could lead to disaster. So in addition to being vigilant about supervision, parents should never allow small children to scream, jump wildly, or play chase or tug-of-war with the dog.

Parents should also teach their children not to run and scream in the event they do get nipped by an overexcited puppy. Instead, the child should roll into a ball, protect his hands and face, and call for help. Teach your dog the command "stop,"

It's not safe to leave puppies and children unattended. You don't want one to accidentally injure the other.

FAST FACT

Training sessions work best if kept short. Puppies can handle 5 to 10 minutes, adult dogs about 15 minutes.

and encourage your child to say the word when it's necessary.

It helps to involve your child in training the puppy, but try to make this fun rather than a chore. Once you teach the puppy the basics of "come," "fetch," and "give," let your children give the dog the same commands. Children may find the "give" (or "drop it") command particularly useful—for example, when the puppy latches on to a treasured toy.

To train your dog to give, say his name first. Then say, "give" or "drop it." At the same time, offer the puppy a toy or a really good food treat that is more exciting than

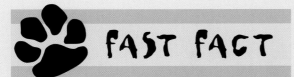

FAST FACT

Training sessions are most effective if they end on a positive note. If you become frustrated during training, don't try to continue until your dog performs the desired behavior. End the session immediately.

what he is holding. The goal is to get the pup to happily relinquish the item.

DOG-PROOFING

It's definitely easier to train your dog if you have the right equipment. Baby gates, doors, exercise pens, and crates are designed to protect your belongings and to separate your dog from areas where you don't want him to be. The idea is to prevent undesirable behaviors from becoming habits.

When you bring a new puppy or dog home, there's housetraining to do and rules to establish. If you limit your dog's access to only a few areas in your home, you'll be able to watch his behavior. Until you know how inquisitive your dog is, close the doors to rooms with furniture, carpeting, or possessions you don't want him to damage. You can also use baby gates to establish barriers.

Secure loose or dangling electrical cords from household appliances, televisions, lamps, or computers to prevent your dog from tripping over or chewing them. Keep clothing, children's toys, important papers, jewelry, and all small objects out of your dog's reach. Once your dog is housetrained and only chews his own toys, you can return these things to their original locations and give your dog more leeway to roam indoors. Until then, don't assume that any item is safe unless it's completely out of your dog's sight. Big dogs can stand on their hind legs or jump up on furniture to reach objects on counters or tables. Some dogs even know how to climb ladders!

Kitchen counters with food are especially vulnerable. Socks or shoes left on the floor are fair game to your dog. When you can't watch your dog, give him some toys and put him in an exercise pen or a crate. It's amazing how much damage a dog can cause when left alone.

CRATE TRAINING

If you think of a crate (or carrier, cage, or den) as a jail, think again. This small, enclosed area is your dog's personal space. But if he's never used a crate before, he may need some training to realize that it's a sanctuary.

Why should you use a crate? As a housetraining aid it's invaluable. Dogs won't go to the bathroom

HOW SMART IS YOUR DOG?

Stanley Coren, a psychology professor at the University of British Columbia and the author of *The Intelligence of Dogs*, believes dogs are more intelligent than many people think. However, canine intelligence is difficult to measure because it differs from human intelligence. For example, one of the three types of dog intelligence, according to Coren, is instinctive intelligence.

Still, there are ways to test a dog's adaptive intelligence, or ability to learn and solve problems. One way to see how your pooch's brain stacks up is to hide something he loves, such as a piece of food or a toy, in a difficult-to-reach spot, such as behind a chair. Watch how he tries to figure out how to retrieve it. If he uses his paws and snout to dig at it and is able to get the item in under a minute, he should go to the head of the class. If he tries to use his snout a few times but gives up, he may be loveable but he's no canine Einstein.

How quickly a dog grasps something you're trying to teach him is another sign of his canine IQ. Coren devised the smile test to measure how readily a dog picks up on human social cues. Sit a few yards away from your dog and stare at his face. Make eye contact and smile at him. Count how many seconds it takes him to come to you with his tail wagging. If he does it within five seconds, he's a star. If he ignores you, either he doesn't like you much or he isn't an A student.

Your dog should feel at ease and happy in his crate, and should not mind when you tell him to get inside.

where they sleep, so they teach themselves to wait until you let them out. Also, when your dog is inside his crate, he can't damage your house, and you know he's in a safe spot.

A couple caveats: A crate is not a babysitter. Nor should it ever be used as a place for punishment.

To train your dog to like his crate, fill it with chew toys and a blanket or cushion. Before putting your dog in his crate, always throw in a biscuit or other food treat such as freeze-dried liver. This will give him an incentive to enter the crate. When he does, close the door.

Stay where he can see you and leave him in the crate for five minutes. Open the door and let him out. Again toss in some treats, let him go inside the crate after them, and close the door for another five minutes. Repeat the process a few more times throughout the day. Gradually increase the time your dog spends inside the crate until he can sleep through the night there.

If your dog needs more enticement to like his crate, feed him his meals there and add cheese spread or peanut butter to the chew toys you put inside with him. Put your dog inside the crate when it's time for him to nap or go to bed at night, when you have to leave the house, or when you are unable to watch him. Never leave your puppy in his crate for longer than four hours during the daytime. Because their bladders are small, puppies can't wait much longer than four hours before having to relieve themselves. They can generally last through most of the night, however.

Training your puppy to use a crate will likely pay off at some point in his life. For example, he might have to spend the night at the veterinarian's office. Or you may want to travel with him on an airplane or take him along with you on vacation. Once he's accustomed to being confined, he'll accept the crate as his home away from home.

CHAPTER FOUR

Teaching the Basics

The relationship between you and your dog is priceless. Once you begin training him to respect your rules, your bond becomes even stronger. From three weeks of age puppies begin absorbing everything they see, hear, smell, taste, and touch. They file away this information in their growing brains. The earlier you begin training your pup, the faster you can become good friends.

If you want to adopt an older dog, remember that it's never too late to begin the training process. It may take a little longer, though.

Before beginning a training session, stock up on treats. Put them in your pocket or store them in a leather pouch attached to your belt.

Involve the entire family in your dog's training. The key to learning is consistency and repetition. Before you know it, he'll understand what you want.

That way you'll be ready to hand out a reward right after your dog does what you want.

When teaching your dog or puppy, first say his name. Then give a clear-cut command, using the same words each time. Above all, don't try to nag your dog to action by repeating a command multiple times. Say it once and wait to allow your dog to think for himself about what you've asked him to do.

While you probably don't want a robotic dog, teaching him the basic obedience commands—such as "sit," "down," "come," "wait," and "stay"— is the foundation for all other types of training. You can use these commands anywhere, including around the house if your dog seems bored or hyperactive.

PAYING ATTENTION

Life is full of distractions. When you take your dog outdoors, anything he sees or sniffs might seem more interesting than you. To facilitate learning and to provide the foundation for teaching your dog the basics, train him to pay attention to you. An upbeat voice, a loving glance, and quick tender touches will always attract his notice.

Whenever he hears you call his name, he should be thrilled that you're interested in him. Around the house, use his name to call him for food, fun, and games. Maintain enthusiastic, happy vocalizations, as dogs are frightened by low, harsh tones. Never call your dog to you for discipline or if you can't reward him for coming.

To get your dog's attention, wait for opportunities indoors when you know it's quiet. In the beginning, avoid training sessions where there are distractions. Don't have other dogs around, answer phone calls, or conduct training while friends are visiting. Choose an isolated space, such as a hallway, where it's easy to keep your dog's attention. Once he responds well to you there, gradually move on to other locations with more distractions. Train him in larger rooms with a little more noise, then in the backyard, and finally in public places.

When you practice with your dog, choose a time before meals when he's getting hungry. Use small food treats that he doesn't routinely receive. Because they can be chewed and swallowed more quickly, soft bits work better than hard bits. You want your dog to be able to refocus his attention without taking much time out to chow down.

Standing in front of your dog, say his name and move a few feet away. When he moves with you, tell him,

WHAT AGE TO START

Puppies are capable of learning anything you teach them on the day you bring them home. A puppy's mind is open to new behaviors, and he'll be eager to please. Just remember to keep the training sessions positive, fun, and short—no more than 5 to 10 minutes per session. Puppies need to know good manners and household rules right away, so don't wait too long to begin training.

As your puppy grows, think of him as an active teenager. He always needs something to do. If you acquire an older dog, he's also capable of learning anything you teach him from the first day he enters your home. Old dogs actually benefit from learning new tricks because these help keep their minds sharp.

"Good boy!" Then quickly hand him a treat. Maintain eye contact with your dog when you give him the goody. Be sure to align the treat between your dog's eyes and yours. Repeat this three to five times in one sequence. Practice a few minutes a day in different locations and with different distractions. Be sure to give him a treat each time. Your dog will soon learn to look at you whenever you say his name—with or without a treat.

USING A CLICKER

Some people opt to train their dogs using a clicker, a small plastic box you hold in the palm of your hand. It has a metal strip that makes a loud clicking sound when you squeeze it.

At the start of clicker training, you click and immediately give your dog a food treat. You repeat this often enough so that your dog thoroughly associates the clicking sound with the reward. After that you can use the clicker to train your dog in other behaviors, but without giving food treats as a reward. The clicking sound itself is the reward.

Dogs can be taught to do just about anything with clicker training. But the technique requires exact timing, and beginners may need to enroll their dogs in a clicker training class to learn the nuances. For this reason, many trainers prefer to say, "yes!" or "good!" instead of using a clicking sound to let the dog know that he's performed the desired behavior.

SIT

Your dog already knows how to sit. Now he just needs to sit when you ask him to. Begin by getting your dog's attention. To do this, hold a piece of food between your thumb and forefinger. Let him sniff and lick it, but don't give it to him. Slowly move your hand up from his nose and over his head. If he jumps up, you're holding the food too high. His head should follow the treat.

Say his name and "sit" (not "sit down"). When his rear touches the ground, quickly pop the treat into his mouth and in an upbeat, happy voice say, "good sit." Let him hold the position for a brief minute. Then release him by saying, "OK." Move a few feet away from him.

He should remain in the sit position until you give the release "OK." If he does get up, repeat the exercise.

DOWN

Teaching your dog how to lie down begins with a sit. Position yourself next to your dog with both of you facing the same direction. While holding a treat, slowly move your hand down toward your dog's front paws and back toward you.

Teaching your dog the "down" command comes in handy. You can use it to calm your dog if he's antsy or has to wait.

Tiny pieces of diced cooked chicken make excellent rewards for your dog during training sessions. Other goodies include tidbits of cooked liver or pieces of fresh apple, pear, or banana.

Don't slide the treat forward or your dog's rear will pop up. When he begins to lie down, say, "down." When his elbows hit the floor, give him the treat and say, "good down." Let him remain in this position for a few seconds before releasing him by saying, "OK." Repeat the exercise a few times. Gradually increase the length of time your dog remains in the down position.

COME

Training your dog to come to you whenever you call him is one of the most important lessons you'll ever teach him. The "come" command can even save his life—for example, if he darts into a busy street. Using the tastiest rewards during this training builds a solid foundation for learning. The goal is to have your dog think that the best thing he does is come to you the second you call him.

To teach this exercise, attach your dog's leash to his collar and ask someone to hold him for you. Walk a few feet away from your dog and sit on the ground facing him. Holding a food treat in your hand, call your dog's name in an excited, happy voice, followed by "come."

When the dog pulls forward, have the helper release him. Praise your dog enthusiastically as he runs toward you, and give him the treat. Repeat two or three times. Once your dog knows to come to you when you call him, practice indoors without the leash. Keep treats in little treat containers in a variety of places around the house.

WAIT

There are many times when you want your dog to stop where he is and wait. You'll use this when your dog is forging ahead of you or

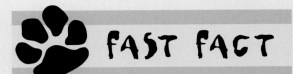

Dogs love games. You can play a fun come-and-go game and at the same time reinforce your dog's training. Show your dog a small food treat, run the other way, and say, "come." Praise him and toss another treat a few feet away from you, saying, "go." When he goes to the treat say, "come" and quickly move away a few feet. Repeat the game a few times.

you're approaching doorways or street corners. To teach this command, walk your dog and, with your left hand gently holding his collar, say, "wait."

Hold your right hand in front of his face and signal him to wait. When you're ready to begin walking again, say, "OK, let's go." Your dog should remain in place until you give him the release command.

STAY

When you tell your dog to stay, he should remain in place until told it's OK to move. Your dog should know the sit command before learning how to stay. Tell your dog to sit. While holding your dog's collar, place a food treat in front of him and say, "stay." Hold on to the collar to prevent him from moving. When he stops pulling, pick up the treat, give it to him, and praise him for staying. Don't let him grab it off the ground or he may think it's OK to pop up.

Repeat several more times, increasing the length of time he remains in place. In the beginning you can expect an average puppy to stay for about 30 seconds. More active pups might only be able to hold the position for 15 seconds.

AWAY FOR TRAINING?

While dropping your dog off at a training school and letting someone else take care of his obedience training might sound like a great idea, think twice before packing his bag. For starters, these schools are more expensive than group classes or private instruction. Plus, the dogs are often left in their kennels when they're not being trained. Dogs are trained without your supervision, and you have no way of knowing what methods the facility is using.

If you do send your dog to a training school, he'll learn to respond to the professional trainer. You'll need to follow the same approach, so the trainer should spend time explaining her methods when you pick up your dog. Often it's the owner, not the dog, who needs the training.

By training the dog yourself, you'll bond with your pet and learn what makes him tick. If he develops a different bad habit later on, you'll know how to handle it without having to call the school. Once you know how to train a dog, you'll be able to use the same methods years later with your second or third dog.

WALKING POLITELY ON A LEASH

One of the greatest pleasures of having a dog is taking him for a walk. He's excited to see the world and just naturally wants to pull ahead. Dogs aren't born knowing how to stroll nicely on a leash, but every dog can be taught to walk beside you instead of ahead of you. For your dog's safety, always take him out on leash. He may spot something interesting across the street and rush into oncoming traffic. Or he might decide to sniff out another dog and wind up in a fight.

To exercise outdoors he'll need a good collar and sturdy leash. There are many kinds from which to choose. A retractable leash is generally not advisable, especially with larger breeds. Your dog will automatically pull on a retractable leash, and you may find it very difficult to control him if an aggressive dog approaches. Also, the elastic cord can easily become tangled around a dog's body parts or yours and cause injury. Instead, use a four-to-six-foot leash.

Flat buckle or snap collars are easy to use. However, dogs usually

One of the most basic, but important, skills your dog can learn is how to walk on a leash properly. Teaching your dog to behave while out in public will make walks more enjoyable for both of you.

pull harder on these types of collars, and some dogs can slip their heads out and escape. A choke chain collar is very effective in preventing strong dogs from pulling, but you will need some training to use it properly. Head halters or head collars must be fitted to your dog and are effective

Every dog/owner combination will have a preference with regard to leashes and collars. Some owners find that a body harness gives them more control over a larger breed like this Labrador Retriever. Try a few different styles and see what works best for you.

in reducing pulling, although some dogs dislike them and they can cause irritation.

Front-clip or body harnesses can be used right away, but some dogs pull even more with these. Other types of harnesses are designed to prevent pulling. When the dog pulls on a harness there's no pressure on the throat, but the chest takes the weight. A canine body harness can be used instead of a collar and fastens with adjustable straps across the dog's chest and behind his front legs. The leash is attached to a D-ring on the strap across the dog's back.

Begin teaching your dog how to walk politely by first telling him to sit so you can calmly put on his leash. Hold the leash in your right hand close to your waist. With your dog on your left side, the leash should cross over your legs. You can use your left hand to grab the leash halfway down between your waist and your dog's neck to take sudden control if necessary.

Once the leash is clipped on, your dog should wait and allow you to go out the door first. In the beginning, take him to an area without a lot of distractions. When he learns the basics of walking without pulling, you can take him places with other people and dogs.

Begin walking. When he moves forward with you, say, "yes!" Immediately give him a small food treat. If he pulls ahead, simply stop walking and wait. Be patient. It may take your dog a few sessions to figure out that pulling the leash is unacceptable. He'll eventually understand what you're teaching him.

CHAPTER FIVE

Housetraining 101

No one likes a piddling puppy in the house, and doggy doo-doo is far from welcome on the good carpet. But just because your dog has bathroom issues doesn't mean that you have to accept them.

It's actually very easy to teach a dog of any age to do his business where you want him to go. Just put housetraining on the top of your priority list and be extremely diligent and patient during the training process. Until he is fully house-trained, never let your new dog roam the house unsupervised.

The key to housetraining is keeping an eye on your dog the whole time he's awake or putting him in a crate or small confined area when you can't watch him. This prevents mistakes. The more times your dog piddles or poops in

One method of housetraining your dog involves the use of a crate. Because dogs don't like to "go potty" where they sleep, crate training makes them wait to eliminate.

the house, the harder it will be to housetrain him.

There are some other tricks of the trade that make the process much easier. Once you commit to using them, you'll have a dog that knows what going outside is all about.

USING A CRATE

Dogs hate to mess where they sleep. By using a crate, you'll help your dog develop the bowel and bladder control he needs for housetraining. Putting him in a crate for four hours or less during the daytime can prevent him from eliminating. When you take him out and directly to the potty area, he'll relieve himself.

For dogs that come from puppy mills, a crate may not help because they were probably forced to sleep in their own excrement. These dogs will need a larger confined area, such as a bathroom or laundry room with a baby gate or an exercise pen. Use newspapers or potty pads a distance away from your dog's bed and water dish. Housetraining may be challenging for puppy-mill dogs. You might want to enlist the aid of a qualified professional trainer or a board-certified veterinary behaviorist.

When buying a crate, select one that's large enough so that your dog can lie down comfortably, stand up, and turn around. The crate shouldn't be so big that there's a lot of empty space behind him, however. If there is, block off the back with cardboard boxes. Any type of crate will do—wire, plastic, or soft-sided.

PICKING A POTTY AREA

Choose an area of the yard near the house where you want your dog to eliminate. When it's time to take him out of his crate, put his leash on and walk him to that spot. Stand still and resist the urge to walk around. Your dog will sniff the area. When he's exhausted all of the new smells, he'll eliminate there.

For the first two or three days, leave his elimination so he will identify his territory and return to the same location next time. After that, keep his area clean. Dogs, like people, don't like to use a dirty potty area.

MAKING A SCHEDULE

Now it's up to you to follow your dog's natural schedule and take him

FAST FACT

You can expect an occasional accident even after your dog is housetrained. If you don't see your dog actually messing in the house, don't scold him after the fact. Just quietly clean up the mess.

USING THE SAME AREA IN THE YARD

You can train your dog to eliminate in the same area in the yard, but it takes some patience. Begin as soon as you bring your new puppy or dog home. Attach his leash to his collar and take him to the designated area. Give him the command "hurry, hurry" and remain in the same spot.

Your dog will sniff the surrounding area, and when he's finished sniffing, he'll accomplish the act. Resist the urge to let your dog wander. This just encourages him to discover new aromas, and he'll forget what he's there to do.

to the potty place when he's ready to eliminate. Puppies younger than four months of age have tiny bladders. While they're awake, they can't hold their urine for longer than about 30 to 45 minutes. They may need 12 to 14 potty breaks every day.

Older pups and dogs will need to eliminate once every two to three hours. Smaller-breed dogs may need to go more often than larger ones. But all dogs need to eliminate when they wake up in the morning, after they eat, after a nap, and after playtime or exercise. It's up to you to take your dog outside at these times.

Establish set times when you will feed, exercise, put your dog in his crate for a nap, and take him out of the crate. This schedule lends predictability to housetraining, and your dog will become accustomed to waiting. It helps to jot down the times when he eliminates so you can establish a pattern. This makes it easier to take him out at the right times.

FAST FACT

For cleaning up doggy accidents inside the home, enzymatic cleaners work better than regular rug shampoos or household cleaners. That's because enzymatic cleaners contain bacteria that digest the pet mess, which will discourage your dog from eliminating in the same spot again.

WATCH AND GIVE CUES

When you take your dog to the potty area, watch him carefully. You'll notice that he sniffs the ground intently, walks in circles, or just stops in his tracks. These signs will let you know that your pup will poop or pee in a few seconds. When you see this behavior, give your dog a verbal cue. Use two or three words that you aren't likely to say around the house to other members of the family, as this may confuse your pooch. "Hurry, hurry" or "do it now" would work well.

Eventually your dog will associate these words with the activity and will relieve himself when you repeat the phrase. This comes in handy in bad weather or when you take your dog on vacation and he feels disoriented because he can't locate his familiar smells.

As soon as he finishes, praise him softly. Bring him back into the house because potty time isn't playtime, especially during the middle of the night.

BE VIGILANT

Your mission is to ensure that your dog doesn't have a chance to make a mistake inside the house. For this reason, watch your dog carefully when he is out of his crate or confined area indoors. If you see the signs that he needs to use the potty, whisk him out the door as quickly as possible, even if he's midstream. When he goes in the designated area, praise him.

If you miss the moment and your dog piddles or poops indoors,

resist the urge to scold your puppy. Above all, don't rub his nose in the accident. This only encourages him to relieve himself indoors in a quiet corner or behind the furniture when

Observe your dog when he looks for his selected "spot." Learning which behaviors signal elimination is imminent can help you prevent accidents inside the house.

RINGING A BELL

Once your puppy understands the basics of housetraining, teach him to ring a bell to let you know when he needs to go out. Hang a string of bells from a cord around the door handle. Make sure it's just long enough for your dog to reach with his nose or paw. Every time you take your dog outside, ring the bells. The idea is for your dog to associate the bell ringing with going outdoors to eliminate.

If your dog nudges the bells or sniffs them, praise him and open the door. When he taps the bells with his paw or nose, reward him lavishly and take him outside immediately. Be consistent, and soon your dog will ring the bells when he wants to go outside.

you're not looking. Instead, get a paper towel and take your pup back to the accident spot. Blot the pee or pick up the poop in the paper towel, then take it, along with your pup, outside to the potty area. Smear the pee or drop the poop in the area, then step back and calmly praise your pup as though he had gone in the right place to begin with. Afterward, put your puppy back in his crate or play area and thoroughly clean area where he messed with an enzymatic cleaner. View the accident as a wake-up call to be more vigilant next time.

NIGHTTIME TRAINING

Even young puppies can housetrain themselves at night. Right before your bedtime, take your pup outdoors. When he's finished, put him inside his crate and say, "good night." It helps if the crate is next to your bed so you can hear him if he needs to go outside during the night.

If he does wake up and whine to go outside, take him out quickly. But do not talk or play with him. Then return him to his bed. He'll realize that going outside in the middle of the night is for business only and not an opportunity to escape the crate and have fun.

FAST FACT

If your dog has repeated accidents after he's housetrained, it's possible that he has a medical condition. Take him to the veterinarian for a checkup.

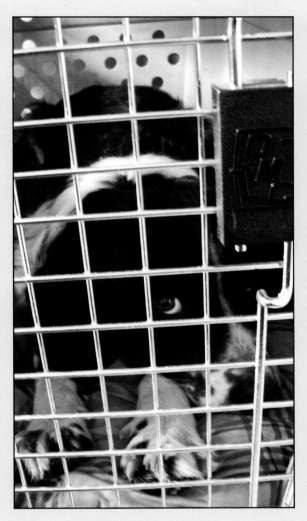

Check your dog's bedding every day to make sure he hasn't had an accident. He'll house-train faster if his bedding is clean.

PATIENCE COUNTS

Housetraining doesn't happen overnight. The process takes time, patience, and understanding. Some breeds catch on to the training faster than others. In addition, your puppy or adult dog may have formed bad habits in his previous home that will take longer to correct.

When you begin taking your dog outside to do his business, be prepared to wait a bit. If you know that he's due to go but doesn't eliminate within five minutes, take him back into the house and put him in his crate or confined area for 15 minutes. Then take him out and try again.

Many new owners complain that when housetraining, they stay outside for a long time futilely waiting for their dog to eliminate. Then, as soon as they bring the dog indoors, he goes there. For dogs that have a difficult time learning where to do their business, try using small tasty food treats as rewards when they eliminate outdoors.

CHAPTER SIX

Preventing Problem Behaviors

Sometimes a good dog or puppy can do a bad thing. What this means is that he needs more training or a different type of training so he can correct his behavior. Some problem behaviors, such as submissive urination or escaping through doorways, are easy to correct. Others, like aggression or severe separation anxiety, will take more time.

The trick to fixing a problem behavior is to detect what's causing it. Find out what your dog is really

It's OK for a puppy to bark during play, but constant barking is a nuisance that must be stopped.

thinking and what prompts him to react this way. Once you figure this out, you can work toward finding a solution. For severe issues that defy detection, don't hesitate to contact a veterinary behaviorist or qualified professional trainer for help.

Neutering your male dog or spaying your female dog may make training easier. While it doesn't eliminate the "teenage" rebellious behavior that most dogs go through, it should help to some degree, depending upon the breed and individual temperament.

AGGRESSION

A dog is aggressive for a variety of reasons. These include his genetics, how his mother and breeder raised him, his relationship with his littermates, the type of early learning he received, diet, physical and mental health, and life experiences. While many forms of aggression can be managed and controlled through good training and positive learning experiences, some cases require professional help.

Aggression covers a wide range of behaviors. It usually begins slowly and builds to an attack. Some owners might not recognize the early warning signs of aggression. They think their dog suddenly flies into a rage. The fact is, however, that an aggressive dog always gives some type of warning, even a minor one, before biting.

Learn to recognize your dog's body language for cues into his behavior. A curl of the lips is a snarl. A hardening of the eyes is a defiant stare. Ears pulled back indicate fear. Alert all people who interact with your dog to be alert and avert potential bites. Avoid confronting an aggressive dog with more aggression, as this only escalates the problem.

BARKING

More than large dogs, many small dogs love to bark out of excitement or boredom. The best way to train your dog not to bark is to train him to "talk," or bark on command and then stop barking when you tell him, "quiet." The next time your dog barks when someone knocks on the door, give him the command

FAST FACT

According to some holistic veterinary practitioners, pheromone sprays can curtail stress-related problem behaviors like excessive barking. Squirted in a room, vehicle, or crate, these sprays may relax a dog and give him a sense of well-being.

"talk." When it's quiet tell him to "talk" again. If he barks on command, praise him and give him a treat.

The next step is to give him the "talk" command, then tell him "quiet" and reward him with food and praise. Alternate the commands until your dog can follow your instructions. The next time he barks, you tell him to be quiet and reward him for obeying instead of yelling at him for barking.

If your dog barks when you're away, it probably means that he's bored or lonely. When you leave, make sure to give him some toys stuffed with food to help relieve his loneliness and boredom. Consider hiring a dog walker or dog sitter to visit him while you're gone. Tiring him out before you leave helps too. Play a vigorous game of fetch or take your dog out for a walk or a run before you leave.

CAR TRIPS

Begin taking your dog on short car trips around town as soon as you bring him home. Some dogs get carsick and need time to adjust to the motion. Try giving your dog a few gingersnap cookies about a half-hour before you take him in the car. Also, don't feed him a large meal before leaving. Always use a doggy seat belt

to protect him while riding, and have him face forward. Leave the window open a little to give him some fresh air. Never let your dog hang his head out the window. Something could fly into his eyes, nose, or ears and cause injury.

If your dog is overly nervous about riding in the car, desensitize him gradually. First, sit inside the car with your dog. Turn the radio on, but don't start the engine. The next time, start the engine and back the car out a few feet before returning to your starting point. When your dog gets used to this, drive short distances. Eventually you'll be able to take your pooch on longer trips.

CHEWING

Pups love to chew just about anything that feels good on their gums and has an enticing odor. To your dog it doesn't matter if this happens to be your favorite shoes, the mail, your wallet, or your expensive sunglasses. The surest way to prevent losing your possessions is to put them out of your dog's reach.

Close the doors or use baby gates to block off rooms of the house that you don't want your dog to enter. As soon as you bring your dog home, give him interesting toys to chew on so he sticks to his own things. Stuff a few of his toys with

Your puppy will chew just about anything he can fit in his mouth. Take the proper precautions to ensure he can't reach items that are valuable or potentially harmful.

food and rotate his toys so that he continually has new things to keep his interest.

DIGGING AND YARD DESTRUCTION

If a dog wants to bury a treasured item, unearth a rodent, investigate interesting-smelling tree roots, or find a cool resting place, he won't hesitate to dig. Any dog can feel the urge to dig up the dirt, though terriers that were bred to hunt under-

ground prey are more prone to digging than other breeds.

To discourage your dog from digging, provide a shaded area where he can cool off, or buy him a doggy outdoor cot on which to nap. Another alternative is to create a digging pit just for him. Set aside one area of the yard and fill it with loose dirt or sand. Surround it with low fencing or stones. Bury a few of his treasured bones or toys just below the surface of the dirt there. Entice him to the spot by digging a little there yourself. When he follows your lead, praise him. A few days later, bury a few more items and visit the area. Create a fun game of digging with your dog and soon he'll choose this area over the rest of the yard.

If you see your dog digging in another area, get his attention by clapping your hands sharply. Then redirect him to the digging pit. The message is that it's not fun to dig elsewhere.

Protect your plants or vegetable garden by putting up garden fencing around sensitive areas. Motion-activated devices that emit loud alarms or turn on a water hose can also deter your dog from digging.

Don't take your dog to a spot where he's previously dug a hole and reprimand him. He won't understand why you're yelling at him. Above all, don't fill the hole with water and hold his head underwater. This is inhumane and may cause him to react aggressively.

A dog that insists on digging should be given a spot in the yard where this activity is permitted.

If your dog is digging at the fence to escape the yard, bury concrete blocks a few inches below the fence line. Dogs don't like the way concrete feels on their nails. Wireless fencing might seem like a good solution, but often it doesn't work. Dogs that are intent on getting out of the yard will endure a shock when they approach the perimeter. If they decide to come back, they get shocked again, which will only encourage them to stay away.

JUMPING UP

No one likes a dog leaping up at them, yet this is what some highly sociable but untrained dogs love to do when they meet someone. Preventing this behavior is a lot easier than curing it. Begin by telling your dog to sit whenever a stranger approaches. While he's in a sitting position, bend down and give him a treat.

For an overenthusiastic dog that has trouble sitting outdoors when greeting someone, put your foot on the leash when he jumps up. When he's in the sitting position, reward him with a treat and praise.

Another way to fix the problem is to cross your arms on your chest and stand still without making eye contact with your dog. When he jumps, turn around and ignore him. When he doesn't receive any atten-tion from you, he'll lose interest in jumping on you. Kneeing him in the chest can be painful and is not an effective way to change this type of behavior.

MOUTHING

When playing, your puppy will tend to grab things with his mouth. When those things include your hands or feet, playtime can turn painful. Unfortunately, puppies aren't born knowing that their bite can hurt. To get your puppy to be gentle, let him mouth your hand. But when he bites too hard, give a high-pitched "yeow," which signals that you're hurt. Then relax your hand completely. This will surprise him and he'll stop. If he repeats the mouthing, cry out "yeow" again.

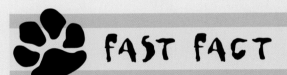

FAST FACT

A variety of household products and plants can be toxic to dogs if ingested. If you suspect that your dog has swallowed a poisonous substance, contact your veterinarian immediately or call the ASPCA Animal Poison Control Center at (888) 426-4435. The center is open 24 hours a day, 365 days a year. The following Web site offers information about common poisonous plants and other toxins: www.aspca.org/pet-care/poison-control.

Repeat once or twice more. If your puppy continues mouthing after that, remove your hand and ignore or move away from him. Wait a bit, then play with him again. Repeat the process. If he mouths you again, cry out and stop playing. Eventually he'll understand that he loses your body part when he bites too hard. He'll be a kinder, gentler puppy.

If your puppy becomes too excited and bites when you pet or touch him, distract him from this behavior by offering some small food treats from your other hand. If he bites your feet, keep his favorite chew toy handy. When he goes for your lower extremities, wave the toy at him.

Mouthing or gnawing on hands is a puppy habit that should be eliminated.

If your puppy is out of control, think sleep. He's probably tired and needs to go into his crate for a nap. Other solutions to mouthing include supplying your dog with several enticing toys to encourage him to play with those instead of using you as a chew toy. Socialize him outdoors with other dogs and people so your body parts are not his only form of exercise. You can also use an unpleasant-tasting spray such as Grannick's Bitter Apple on your hands and clothing before you interact with him.

Be sure to praise your dog when he goes to mouth you and thinks twice about it. Be patient, as changing this behavior takes time. Above all, don't slap your dog or jerk your hands or feet away when he mouths. This will only encourage him to jump forward and bite again.

PULLING ON THE LEASH

A few techniques will stop your dog from yanking you down the street. Try standing perfectly still when you feel tension on the leash. Or walk a short distance, stop, and offer him a small food treat when you call him back to you. Another way is to surprise him by immediately turning in the opposite direction. Take a few steps forward or backward and make a sharp turn to the right or left.

Repeat the erratic pattern several times in different directions. When he's completely puzzled, he'll pay attention to your body cues instead of forging ahead on his own.

When your dog pulls, don't encourage him by running after him. Do keep the leash loose. When the leash is too short and too tight, there's constant tension on the collar, which encourages pulling.

SEPARATION ANXIETY

For many dogs raised in puppy mills or adopted from shelters, becoming separated from their owners is highly stressful. As young puppies these dogs didn't receive enough attention or proper socialization, and they're fearful they will be abandoned. Other reasons for separation anxiety include being given to a new owner, an abrupt change in schedule, moving to a new location, or the sudden absence of a family member.

If dogs miss out on early socialization from an important person or group of people, they tend to display a variety of destructive behaviors when their owners are gone for even

If you regularly come home to find things broken and chewed in your home, there's a good chance your dog is experiencing separation anxiety.

a short time. They may bark, chew, urinate, defecate, pace, or try to escape from windows, doors, or the yard. These behaviors may be symptoms of distress, but they may also mean that a dog simply needs to learn house manners. It might take some detective work to figure out whether your dog has separation anxiety or some other behavior problem.

For mild cases of separation anxiety, try counterconditioning. This alters the dog's fear, anxiety, or aggression and replaces it with a pleasant reaction. Teach the dog to associate the negative situation with a positive one. Gradually he learns that what he's afraid of actually produces what he loves. If your dog carries on every time you leave the house, give him a toy filled with food that will take him 20 to 30 minutes to finish. Soon he'll look forward to your leaving because he knows he'll receive a delicious treat. Reserve these toys for your departures. If your dog has a moderate case of separation anxiety, this may not work because he may refuse to eat while you're gone.

For moderate or severe cases, condition your dog to being left alone, beginning with a few seconds at a time. Also, teach him that when you pick up your keys you might not be leaving. Sit down for a while. This reduces his anxiety because the

CALLING IN AN EXPERT

If your dog has serious behavioral problems, such as aggression toward people or other animals, phobias, or separation anxiety, you may need more help than obedience classes or private instruction can provide. Another option is to consult with an animal behaviorist. An applied animal behaviorist is an expert in animal behavior and has received specialized training. A certified applied animal behaviorist (CAAB) may be a veterinarian who has completed a residency program in animal behavior.

Applied animal behaviorists have expertise in diagnosing the causes of—and in treating—all sorts of abnormal behavior. In some cases these specialists will work directly with the dog owner to implement a treatment plan. In other cases they may recommend medications, such as tranquilizers or antidepressants, for the veterinarian to prescribe.

You can locate a certified applied animal behaviorist by asking your veterinarian or by looking online at www.certifiedanimalbehaviorist.com.

departure cues he's become accustomed to dreading won't always signal that you're leaving. Eventually he won't be so anxious when he sees them.

You can also take your pooch to doggy daycare, or ask a friend or dog sitter to stay with your dog while you're gone. Be sure to give him plenty of exercise when you are home, and sign him up for a positive-training class to build his self-esteem. Whatever you do, don't punish or scold your dog for behavior stemming from his separation anxiety, as this makes the problem worse. He's not being disobedient when he acts out in your absence. He's genuinely frightened and is desperately trying to cope with his fear.

STOOL EATING

Sometimes a puppy or dog defecates and then eats all or some of his excrement. This behavior, called coprophagia, could be caused by separation anxiety or a lack of digestive enzymes and B vitamins in his diet. While stool eating doesn't pose a serious health problem to your dog, it's unpleasant to watch.

The best way to discourage this habit is to clean up your dog's stool as soon as he leaves it. If it's not around, he can't go after it. Try adding digestive enzymes as a daily supplement to his food to help with digestion and nutrient absorption, or change his food to a high-quality or balanced home-cooked recipe.

SUBMISSIVE URINATION

If your housetrained dog urinates all over the floor when you or your guests walk in, it's frustrating and embarrassing. Puppies—especially shy, timid, and insecure ones—and recently adopted dogs that become overly excited may produce dribbles of urine or large puddles. Most dogs outgrow the problem by one year of age, though some dogs never do.

To help manage the problem, ignore your dog when you first walk in the door. Give him a few minutes to relax before interacting with him. Resist the urge to make eye contact with him. Sit on the floor next to him or squat down, but don't stand over your dog and bend toward him, as this makes him feel more inferior. Pet him under the chin or on the chest rather than over the top of his

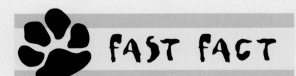

FAST FACT

If your senior dog begins to have more bathroom accidents, there may be a medical reason. Take him to the veterinarian for an evaluation.

PROBLEMS WITH OLDER DOGS

As dogs age, they begin to lose some of their abilities. Their sense of sight and hearing diminishes, and their awareness of their surroundings begins to lessen. Their sleep cycles change, causing them to sleep more during the day and be more active at night. Other signs of aging include wandering aimlessly, staring at objects, and even forgetting housetraining and house rules. At some level dogs may be aware of the changes they're experiencing, but they don't understand why these changes are happening. This increases their anxiety level and may cause them to react more aggressively than they once did.

Continuing to play with your dog, providing exercise, and giving him opportunities to learn new behaviors will help keep his mind sharp and maintain physical fitness. Like people, dogs benefit from keeping their brains and their bodies active.

head. If he begins to urinate, don't yell or punish him. Simply clean it up without saying anything.

Frequent urination may also have medical causes. Schedule a checkup with the veterinarian to rule out a urinary tract infection. Other reasons for bathroom accidents include incomplete housetraining or wanting to mark the territory.

CHAPTER SEVEN

Competing in Dog Sports

Dogs love nothing better than hanging out near the food bowl or running after birds in the yard, but there's more to life than this. Getting out of the house, sniffing other four-legged friends, and participating in organized dog sports can make for good, clean fun. Training a dog to jump over hurdles, whip through a tunnel, or follow obedience directions to sit, stay, or lie down has other bonuses.

When you teach your dog the ins and outs of outdoor events, it boosts the bond between the two of you. It also gives your dog an opportunity to exercise his mind as well as his body. Staying busy reduces boredom and subsequent behavior problems as well.

Agility trials provide good exercise and great fun for a dog.

Today mixed-breed and purebred dogs can participate in American Kennel Club (AKC) performance events. With training, patience, and practice, your dog can easily excel at these events, even if he's not the most athletic member of his species.

Before getting involved in any sports with your dog, make sure he's in good condition. Schedule an appointment with your veterinarian to assess your dog's fitness level. The checkup should include an evaluation of your dog's heart, lungs, joints, ligaments, and weight.

If your dog is overweight, hold off on strenuous workouts. Instead, start walking him a few more minutes each day. Add time as he takes off some weight and builds his stamina. Put him on a diet by cutting down slightly on his regular food. Feel free to add a few grated and steamed fruits and veggies to his meals if he seems extra-hungry. Dogs love apples, carrots, string beans, broccoli, and zucchini.

DOG CAMPS

For an introduction to different canine sports, consider attending a dog camp with your dog. Held in various locations throughout the United States, dog camps are a great way to explore new canine performance activities and vacation at the same time. Here you'll receive instruction in a relaxed environment. You'll also have the opportunity to make new friends who care about having a good time with their dogs. Depending on the facility, camp experiences may include hiking, flyball, swimming, lure coursing, carting, freestyle, obedience, and agility. Many offer games, safety seminars, trick training, and group campfires.

Camps generally accept puppies to senior dogs, and they welcome purebred and mixed-breed canines alike. Many camps sponsor educational events and invite well-known dog trainers and behaviorists, who offer instruction in the latest training methods.

A good canine camper gets along well with other dogs. He should already know the five basic commands of sit, stay, down, come, and

FAST FACT

Long nails can easily become snagged on objects and will tear during sports. To avoid injury, keep your dog's nails as short as possible. If your dog has dewclaws, trim or protect them by wrapping the nail and the surrounding area with Vet Wrap, a stretchy bandage that sticks to itself.

easy. These will come in handy when you're training your dog to take his athletic abilities to the next level.

AGILITY

Picture your dog having the time of his life scaling an A-frame, zooming around curves, balancing on a see-saw, and leaping through a tire. These are only a few of the obstacles in agility competition. Created in England, agility is the hottest canine sport in the United States—and with good reason.

Breeds of all sizes and shapes, their owners, and spectators love this fast-paced, exhilarating activity. Handlers guide their dogs through a complex obstacle course that includes going up and across a three- or four-foot-high plank, weaving in and out of a series of poles, jumping over and through objects, and swooshing through tunnels.

FAST FACT

High-performance dogs need more protein and fat in their diet to maintain their energy levels and muscle mass. Choose a recipe containing a higher percentage of these ingredients rather than just increasing the amount of your dog's food.

In agility competitions, dogs are measured for speed and accuracy. They compete in their own height divisions and can earn nine AKC agility titles. Organizations that sponsor agility trials include the AKC, the United States Dog Agility Association (USDAA), the Australian Shepherd Club of America (ASCA), and the North American Dog Agility Council (NADAC).

If your dog already reliably responds to the five basic commands, you can get started in agility by signing up for a class. Watch out: agility classes can be addictive! You'll learn how to train your dog to follow your verbal and nonverbal cues, from both your right and left sides. With patience and lots of practice, you and your dog can become a tightly knit team.

Even if you decide not to compete, the agility courses are fun to

FAST FACT

Puppies should not participate in strenuous exercise such as jogging, jumping, or running alongside a bicycle. Wait until your dog is two years old before beginning these activities. Before then his bones are not fully formed and are prone to damage if stressed.

run. Plus, they provide good mental stimulation for you and your dog.

DOCK JUMPING

If your purebred or mixed-breed dog loves the water and enjoys chasing moving objects—and if you don't mind getting wet—then dock jumping might be a good canine sport to consider. The sport builds trust and

This dog is participating in the "Extreme Vertical" portion of the Iron Dog Competition. This is a variation on dock jumping.

confidence between dog and owner. Adults, teens, and children as young as six can participate. Dock-jumping competitions are held throughout the United States during the summer months.

There are several forms of dock jumping, but all start with a 40-foot-long dock at a lake or attached to a large aboveground pool. The canine competitor races down the dock and leaps into the water in pursuit of a favorite toy. Two sponsoring organizations, DockDogs and Splash Dogs, offer titles in three competitions: Air, Vertical, and Speed Retrieve. In the Air competition, the length the dog jumps is measured from the edge of the dock to the point where the dog's tail hits the water. For Vertical, dogs launch off the dock into the air, trying to grab a toy bumper in their mouth. Ropes above the water suspend the toy, and the dogs are scored on how high they jump to grab it. In Speed Retrieve the dogs dive off the dock and swim out to grab a realistic-looking foam pheasant or duck suspended two inches above the water.

Practicing may be a challenge because of the dearth of regulation dock-jumping facilities. But if you live near a lake with a dock, you're all set for splashdown. Teamwork, diet, and conditioning are the foundations for dock-jumping success.

To get started, play with your dog's favorite toy on land. Encourage him to chase it while you're holding it. Raise the toy higher in the air, but keep asking him to go after it. Be sure to praise him when he does jump. Now you're ready for the shoreline. This time, stand in the water and hold the toy in front of you so he has to jump to reach it. Praise him for his effort. Repeat the exercise, standing a little farther back and holding the toy up higher.

FLYBALL

Blink and you'll miss your dog racing from the start line, leaping over a set of hurdles, stepping on a spring-loaded pad and releasing a tennis ball, catching the ball, and sprinting back to the start line. Welcome to the wonderful world of flyball. It's one fast sport, with dogs reaching nearly 30 miles per hour on the course.

Flyball consists of a four-dog relay team. Four hurdles are placed 10 feet apart down a 51-foot line. Each dog must release a ball from the box, catch it, and return it across the line back to the start. All four dogs on the team must cross the finish line to win a heat. Penalties are assessed if a ball is dropped or the next relay dog is released early.

Because of the physical demands of this sport, canine athletes need to be in top physical shape. You'll need to provide a good diet with a little more protein content. You'll also need to condition your dog to achieve racing fitness.

To get started, join a flyball training class. Dogs must wear flat collars; slip collars and leads are not permitted.

The "restrained recall" is the key concept in flyball. It is essential that

A small dog races over hurdles during a flyball competition. To be successful at flyball, a dog must be fast, agile, and smart.

GAMES DOGS PLAY

If you'd rather not get involved in organized dog sports, you can always play games with your dog. They're a great way to strengthen the human-canine bond, keep your dog physically active, and stimulate his brain to learn new things. The games should be fun, with simple rules that are easy to follow.

Everyone knows about fetch. Toss a tennis ball as far as you can and ask your dog to go get it. Retrievers love this one, but any dog can be taught to return an object.

Especially good for a rainy day, playing hide-and-seek sharpens your dog's recall and reassures him that coming to you when you call is always a good idea. While indoors, give him a "sit" or "down wait" command. Then hide behind the couch or inside a closet. When you're ready, use a squeaky toy or call him. Give him a treat and praise him when he finds you. Repeat the game by using the same hiding spot. Add new locations when your dog takes less time to find you.

Another game you can play with your dog—one that actually helps you tidy up the house at the same time—is "clean up your toys." Push your dog's toys into a small area. Ask your dog to pick up one of the items and place it in your hand. Give him a food treat when he does what you've asked. Then drop the toy in a box. Ask your dog to give you another item. When he places it in your hand, reward him again and drop the item in the box. Some dogs will shorten the process by dropping the toy into the box themselves.

you teach your dog to return to you, his owner. When training your dog, you'll need a helper to hold him while you walk away. The goal of the exercise is to have your dog pull toward you. When you call his name, the helper should release him and he should run to you. Put your hands on your dog's collar before giving him a treat. When your dog can perform this at 30 or 40 yards away, you're ready to add some speed: run away from him and make him chase you.

Learning how to jump hurdles is the next step. Dogs must learn to do this while avoiding the distraction of other dogs running the other way. Once your dog can manage this trick, he's ready to learn how to step on the front pedal of the box that releases the tennis ball. Praise the dog when he has possession of the ball.

FLYING DISC

Watching a dog chase after and leap into the air to catch a flying disc is a sure crowd pleaser. But it's also great fun for dog and owner. In flying disc events, mixed-breeds and purebreds compete individually or on teams. Medium-sized dogs have an easier time with this sport than do very small or very large dogs. Dogs with back problems should never participate. Leaping up in the air and landing on the ground can be hard on the back, as well as elbows, knees, shoulders, and feet. Always check with your veterinarian before getting involved.

There are two primary types of flying disc competition:

distance/accuracy and freestyle. In the former, dogs are scored on how far they go to catch a disc and how many discs they successfully catch and return in a given time. Freestyle involves more elements in a choreographed routine, such as multiple discs thrown at the same time and showy jumps.

To train your dog for flying disc, teach him to sit and wait until you give the go-ahead to catch the disc. Training for competition will stimulate your dog's natural prey drive. Getting some dogs to relinquish the disc once they've caught it can be a

Dogs can easily be taught how to catch a flying disc or ball.

HOT-WEATHER PRECAUTIONS

Other than dock jumping and water sports, avoid participating in outdoor activities with your dog during very hot weather. Dogs can easily become overheated and dehydrated. The signs of dehydration are excessive panting, lethargy, and bloodshot eyes. Overweight dogs and those with darker coats are particularly susceptible to sunstroke as they absorb more heat. Flat-faced breeds such as Bulldogs, Boston Terriers, Boxers, and Pugs are especially at risk because they can't get enough air to circulate through their short nasal passages.

Keep your dog cool by only exercising early in the morning, late in the afternoon, or during the early evening hours. During hot weather avoid walking or exercising your dog on concrete, macadam, or asphalt; the temperatures on these surfaces can soar and burn your dog's feet.

When exercising, always bring along a container of cool, fresh water for your dog to drink. Collapsible or non-spill containers work well. If your dog doesn't feel like drinking, pour some water on a towel and let him stand on it. To cool your dog off quickly, pour some water on his chest, belly, and groin areas, plus the pads of his feet. These spots absorb moisture.

Dogs should never be left alone in a vehicle, especially in the summer. The car's temperature can quickly rise, causing your dog to have a heatstroke. Signs of impending heatstroke include rapid panting, sudden fatigue, a purplish tongue, disorientation, and a body temperature above 105° Fahrenheit (40.5° Celsius). Should you notice any of these symptoms, work fast. Get your dog in the shade and wet her down with cool (not icy) water. Then get her to the vet as quickly as possible. Heatstroke can be fatal if not treated immediately, so take precautions when it's hot outside.

challenge. Take the time to figure out what best motivates your dog to give it to you. Perhaps he'll readily trade it for a food treat. Perhaps he'd prefer a chance to play with a tug toy.

FREESTYLE

In canine musical freestyle, you and your dog dance together in a program set to music. The sport showcases how well the two of you perform intricate, choreographed movements and interpret the theme of the music. Heelwork-to-music blends traditional dog obedience and the art of dressage with music. Both forms thrill crowds of canine lovers and are a joy for dog and handler to perform. Juniors up to 18 years of age and adults compete in various levels of difficulty and can earn titles.

To begin bonding with your dog to music, enroll in a good basic obedience class that prepares you and your dog to earn a Companion Dog (CD) title. Attention training is essential for freestyle, as dogs must heel on all sides of the handler. Locate a freestyle class so you can gain the support of an instructor and other dog dancers and learn the intricacies of the sport.

Once you have a good grasp of the basics, teach your dog to move back in a straight line from the heel position. Train him to pivot in place in the heel position on both sides of you and in front of you. Teach him to sidestep in both directions, on both sides and in front. From there the possibilities of dance movements are endless. Select a piece of music for your routine that fits the natural rhythms of your dog. Then get ready to rock out!

OBEDIENCE

The oldest and most basic of the AKC competitions, competitive obedience, is also the most practical. Everyone appreciates a dog that responds to "sit," "down," and "come," and the training extends to eliminating household nuisance behaviors such as jumping on people, excessive barking, and digging.

Any breed can compete and earn six titles: Companion Dog (CD), Companion Dog Excellent (CDX), Utility Dog (UD), Utility Dog Excellent (UDX), Obedience Trial Champion (OTCh), and National Obedience Champion (NOC).

Start by enrolling your dog in a good competitive obedience class. You'll learn the basics of the sport and the nuances of competition. Set aside some time each week for practice sessions with your dog.

RALLY

The AKC's newest competitive sport for dogs, rally, is a more relaxed version of traditional obedience competition. Dog and handler complete, at their own pace, on a course

FAST FACT

On a 73°F (23°C) day, the temperature inside a car can reach 120°F (49°C) in 30 minutes. On a 90°F (32°C) day, the temperature can reach 160°F (71°C) in less than 15 minutes. If you must leave your dog alone in your vehicle for a short period, keep the air conditioner running or use a window fan (available in pet catalogs and some pet supply stores) to help provide good air circulation.

with 10 to 20 designated stations. Each station has a sign with instructions about the next skill to be performed.

Scoring is more relaxed than in traditional obedience. While the team is expected to move briskly, handlers may talk to their dogs and give other audible signals, such as clapping or snapping fingers. However, handlers may not touch the dog or make physical corrections. Harsh verbal commands or intimidating signals are penalized.

Rally levels with titles include novice, advanced, and excellent. Start by attending a training class. Be prepared to practice at home.

CHAPTER EIGHT

Preparing for Work

All dog breeds were originally bred to perform specific tasks. Today national breed clubs sponsor competitions that test dogs' abilities to do what they were bred to do. You might find training your dog for these events fun and challenging, while your dog will have a chance to sharpen his skills.

Not all canine sports are appropriate for all dogs or all owners. The Iditarod, for example, isn't for beginners—or for Toy Poodles. To decide what canine competition best fits you and your dog, evaluate his breed characteristics and find the closest athletic match. Some breeds can manage physically but may not have

Retrievers have a natural drive to find items and return them to their masters.

the instinct to excel at certain sports. Also consider what you like to do. If you don't really enjoy hunting, don't feel compelled to participate in that activity with your dog.

Once you choose a sport, locate other people in dog clubs and training classes who are willing to share their expertise with you. Check with your breeder. Chances are she's involved in the event you're interested in and can recommend clubs or training classes. She should be able to mentor you too.

Every once in a while, a dog won't be a natural at what his breed was bred to do. Perhaps a Labrador Retriever hates swimming and retrieving, or a Wire Fox Terrier doesn't like to go underground and get his feet dirty. It happens. While your dog may never be able to earn a title in the sport, he may enjoy the practice, or excel at something else.

Whatever canine athletic test you decide to go after, remember that the purpose of being active with your dog is to have something fun to do with him. Don't get so wrapped up in competing that you forget your dog isn't interested in ribbons or titles. All he wants is your love and approval.

EARTHDOG TRIALS

Small terriers and Dachshunds have a chance to test their natural apti-tude when they encounter caged rats underground during Earthdog trials. These tests provide a healthy outlet for excess energy in a controlled situation. Working individually, the dogs are tested at four different levels and may earn three titles: Junior Earthdog (J.E.), Senior Earthdog (S.E.), and Master Earthdog (M.E.).

Dogs begin with an introductory instinct test, called Introduction to Quarry, which is a prerequisite for a title. Dogs must follow a scent to the entrance of a tunnel. They must be willing to enter a dark den and show willingness to work the quarry by barking, digging, growling, lunging, or biting at the bars.

To gauge whether your dog might have any aptitude for or interest in Earthdog trials, take him to a park or other area where there are rabbits, squirrels, or other small animals.

FAST FACT

Earthdogs (terriers and Dachshunds) were originally bred to hunt rats, rabbits, foxes, badgers, and other small animals. These dogs had to be small enough to fit into underground burrows and tenacious enough to fight cornered prey. These dogs were bred with loud barks, so that their owners could find them and dig them up.

When you spot an animal, take your dog to the area and tap the scent line. If he puts his nose to the ground and starts following the scent, he's probably a good candidate for Introduction to Quarry class.

FIELD TRIALS

Some breeds were developed to help their owners supply food for the family table. Pointers and setters searched the fields looking for birds and rabbits. Labrador Retrievers gathered game in the fields. Cocker Spaniels flushed and retrieved game.

FAST FACT

Depending on the breed, the canine olfactory system is 100,000 to a million times more sensitive than that of humans.

While some dogs still help their owners in the same way today, more use their hunting instincts in field trials. At these competitive events, dogs are grouped according to their natural instincts for hunting, following a

Bloodhounds are the canine world's ultimate scent-finders. Their long ears and facial and neck folds sweep along the ground to collect and concentrate scent particles, keeping them near the nostrils. This allows a Bloodhound to pick up a trail weeks after other dogs have given up on it.

scent, or trapping vermin. The dogs compete against one another and earn titles such as Field Champion (FC) and Amateur Field Champion (AFC). There are subgroup trials for retrievers, pointing breeds, and spaniels. Beagles, Basset Hounds, Dachshunds, and Coonhounds have their own trials for trailing game. Each breed or group of dogs is assigned to hunt for a specific type of game, from rabbits and hares to partridges and pheasants.

Beagle field trials consist of three types of trials. In brace, two or three dogs run together and are judged on their accuracy in trailing a rabbit. In small pack option (SPO), the dogs are divided into packs of seven to pursue rabbits. In large pack trials, all the Beagles are free to find and track hares.

Basset Hounds and Dachshunds run separately from one another, although the trials are organized like the Beagle brace trials. Dachshund field trials involve tracking small game through dense brush and alerting handlers to the location of the game.

Pointing breeds hunt in pairs through a course as birds are released. They must find, point to, and retrieve downed birds. The pointing breeds include Brittanys, English Pointers, English Setters, German Shorthaired Pointers, German Wirehaired Pointers, Gordon Setters, Irish Setters, Vizslas, Weimaraners, and Wirehaired Pointing Griffons.

The retrievers must remember, or "mark," the location where birds fell and return the birds to their handlers. Irish Water Spaniels compete in this group. Different levels of difficulty require the dogs to mark multiple birds and locate blind retrieves (unmarked birds). Spaniels must hunt, flush, and retrieve game on land and water. Spaniel breeds eligible for hunt tests include Clumber, Cocker, English Cocker, English Springer, Field, Sussex, and Welsh Springer.

Before beginning your dog's training for field trials, take him to your veterinarian for a checkup to make sure that he's in good condition. Once you have the vet's go-ahead, visit a few field trials without your dog. See if you can envision yourself and your dog participating in this sport. A great way to get started is to earn a working certificate through a breed club. While this is not an official AKC title, it offers an introduction to the sport.

Many professional training operations will get a dog ready for field trials. Most encourage owners to be a part of the daily training, however. They teach owners to train and handle their own dogs in hunt tests and field trials. Some offer private instruction for owners who want to train their own dogs. Many trainers start with basic obedience training and use reward-based motivational training.

HERDING

If you think your dog has a basic instinct to herd livestock, consider getting involved in noncompetitive herding tests. Herding breeds like the Border Collie, Old English Sheepdog, German Shepherd, Rottweiler, Samoyed, and Greater Swiss Mountain Dog can work wonders in moving sheep, goats, or cattle over miles of pasture. These dogs guide their charges through their daily routines. They're tireless workers and an integral part of a rancher's life.

The goal of herding tests is to demonstrate that your dog has the herding skills for which he was bred. The AKC has standardized tests that measure these skills. Although no formal herding training is required, your dog should know how to listen to you before being exposed to other animals.

Introduce your dog to livestock in a pen before exposing him to animals in a pasture. This helps in case your dog wants to run a herd away. Your dog should be exposed to cattle

A Border Collie attempts to intimidate a rebel sheep. Part of a herd dog's duties is to round up stragglers and drive them back to the herd.

TRAINING A SEARCH-AND-RESCUE DOG

Search-and-rescue (SAR) work is arduous, for dog and handler alike. SAR teams routinely trek through rugged wilderness areas or navigate unstable piles of building debris. They find missing persons, search disaster areas for survivors and bodies, and pinpoint crime scene evidence.

SAR dogs typically come from the larger working and sporting breeds, such as the German Shepherd, Doberman, Rottweiler, Golden Retriever, Giant Schnauzer, and Labrador. Purebreds as well as mutts can excel at this work. A SAR dog must be in good physical health and have excellent tracking ability, good listening skills, and a non-aggressive personality.

To dogs, people have a distinctive human smell. Moreover, everyone has a unique scent, and that scent is present in the dead skin cells that we constantly shed. With their extremely sensitive olfactory system, dogs can detect a specific person's scent on an item of clothing, in a vehicle, or on the ground. Some dogs can pick up a scent carried miles through the air. This is why dogs are so good at locating missing persons.

To be an effective SAR team, dog and handler must work very well together. The handler must be expert at reading the dog's signals. The handler must also be proficient in land navigation, wilderness survival, advanced first aid, and CPR.

To gain certification, SAR teams typically train twice a week for a few years. Teams are thoroughly evaluated before being given an assignment. If you're interested, contact an existing SAR unit to begin training. You can locate one through the Web site of the National Association for Search and Rescue (www.nasar.org).

before he takes the AKC's initial Instinct Test. In this test the dog is judged on his ability to move and control livestock by fetching or driving.

LURE COURSING

You wouldn't think that chasing a mechanically operated artificial lure that's actually a white kitchen garbage bag would be so exciting, but to sight hounds such as Afghan Hounds, Greyhounds, Borzoi, and Salukis, it's the cat's pajamas. Sight hounds chase game by sight rather than by scent and are capable of running up to 35 miles per hour. Imitating the coursing of a rabbit or a hare, lure coursing is an exciting sport for hounds and their owners.

Local sight hound clubs host lure-coursing events that are licensed by the AKC and the American Sighthound Field Association (ASFA). If you're thinking about participating in a lure-coursing event, visit one first without your dog so you know what to expect. A dog must attend practice sessions before entering a course, as he may develop the habit of interfering with the trained dogs.

To get started, connect with members of your local sight hound club. They can give you some pointers for practice sessions, which are often held after the lure-coursing trials. Dogs can earn ASFA and AKC titles. In AKC events the hounds are scaled on speed, agility, endurance, overall ability, and follow (pursuit of the lure rather than the other dogs).

TRACKING

The competitive form of canine search and rescue, tracking events are both practical and fun. Dogs and handlers can find lost people or demonstrate how adept they are at finding a scented article, such as a glove left by the tracklayer. The AKC offers tracking tests for all breeds, and a dog only needs to complete one track successfully to earn a title.

Puppies instinctively know how to use their noses. Pups as young as four months of age can begin tracking, although they must be six months of age before they can participate in an AKC tracking test. To get started in tracking, you'll need a harness, a 20-to-40-foot lead, a few flags to mark your track, and an open grassy area away from the road or woods.

Lay a short track with some food tidbits or a toy. At the end of the track, hide a treat under a glove. When your dog finds the treat, praise him and ask him to give you the glove.

Make sure your dog has fun during this activity so he will continue to enjoy the adventure. The AKC offers a Tracking Dog (TD) title, a Tracking Dog Excellent (TDX) title, and a Variable Surface Tracking (VST) title. A Champion Tracker (CT) has passed all three tracking tests.

WORKING DOG TITLES

The AKC, the United Kennel Club (UKC), and other organizations hold specialized events for the following:

CARTING: The dogs help their owners transport small loads in carts. Breeds that participate in this event include the Bernese Mountain Dog, Bouvier des Flandres, Saint Bernard, and Newfoundland.

WEIGHT PULLING: The International Weight Pull Association sanctions competitions that are open to dogs listed with the UKC. Breeds that excel include the Australian Cattle Dog, Alaskan Malamute, Greater Swiss Mountain Dog, Saint Bernard, Samoyed, American Pit Bull Terrier, and American Bulldog.

WATER RESCUE WORK: Newfoundlands and Portuguese Water Dogs are taught to bring floating devices to people and pull them to safety. The dogs are even capable of hauling a boat to land.

CHAPTER NINE

Making Your Dog a Champion

t takes a special canine to be a champion. Watch an American Kennel Club dog show on TV or see one live at county fairgrounds and you'll be dazzled by the parade of purebreds. Dog or conformation shows feature more than 150 breeds and varieties. But at the end of the

With the right training, your dog could become a prize winner!

day, only one winner receives the red, white, and blue rosette emblematic of the Best in Show.

Show dogs must be trained to be competitive in the ring, but they don't need special treatment at home. They're still the same good-natured companions that love napping at your feet or begging for treats. While you can hire a professional handler to train and show your dog, you can also learn how to do it yourself. It just takes time, patience, and lots of practice. In the process, however, you and your dog will have the chance to develop an extraordinarily close and rewarding relationship.

Training for the show ring should be a fun, positive experience. In order to do well, you and your dog have to genuinely like what you're doing. To catch the judge's eye at an exhibition, your dog needs to have attitude and personality to spare. He must enjoy showing off and strutting

FAST FACT

Show dogs don't usually win any money but are given colorful ribbons. Trophies and small gifts such as glassware or photo frames are sometimes awarded to the winners of big events.

his stuff. This is not a sport for insecure or shy dogs that are afraid of people, other dogs or noises, or different places.

To compete in the exhibition ring, your dog must be a purebred that isn't spayed or neutered. Originally, dog shows were created to display breeding stock, and sterilized animals are still ineligible. Your dog should conform to the standard for its breed. The standard—developed by members of the particular breed's national club—is a written description of how the ideal representative of the breed should look, act, and move. Breed standards cover characteristics such as size, color, proportion, structure, and gait.

Before you get carried away with dreams of glory, it's a good idea to ask a breeder or a breed expert to evaluate your dog and explain his attributes and faults. No dog fits the standard perfectly. Successful show dogs come as close as possible.

FAST FACT

The American Kennel Club (AKC) is a purebred dog registry and the largest show-governing body in the United States. The United Kennel Club (UKC) and the American Rare Breed Association (ARBA) also sponsor dog shows.

If good socialization is important for all dogs, it is absolutely essential for show dogs. The show ring is a whirl of sight, sound, and movement. Dogs that compete there must be relaxed, comfortable, and confident around other dogs and around strangers. So if you are considering showing your purebred in the ring, pay special attention to socializing him thoroughly when he is a puppy.

THE RIGHT EQUIPMENT

Show dogs need a few pieces of equipment. These include the following:

SHOW COLLAR AND SHOW LEAD: Once the dog is socialized, he's ready for his show collar and lead. Buckle, snap, or prong collars, harnesses, or head halters are not used in the show ring, so dogs need to behave while wearing a regular slip-type collar and lead. When used correctly, slip-type collars are effective in controlling pulling behavior.

Collars should be two to three inches longer than the dog's neck size. To determine the right size for your dog, take him to the store and try on different collars. You can also buy show collars and leashes at dog shows or through dog supply catalogs or Web sites.

At conformation shows, dogs wear a thin nylon or chain show collar, usually in a color that matches the dog's neck. Handlers use a short leash made of nylon or leather. Most handlers of terrier and toy breeds use a one-piece collar and lead called a Resco.

TRAVEL CRATE: Dogs should travel to shows in a dog carrier. Because there is some downtime at shows while exhibitors are waiting to go

Proper training is a must for dogs that compete in conformation events. Your dog must be able to remain calm and composed while interacting with many unfamiliar people and dogs.

into the ring, the dog will need to rest in his crate from time to time.

It's important that dogs not bark at shows, so they should be trained to accept confinement happily and quietly. There's no dog show rule against barking. It's just a courtesy to other exhibitors.

GROOMING TOOLS: To look their best in the ring, show dogs should be bathed and groomed before the show. Depending upon the breed's coat type, the dog needs to accept brushing or combing, as well as having his teeth brushed and his nails clipped.

ENROLL IN A CLASS

A good way for your dog to learn the show basics is to take him to conformation classes. To locate a class, contact your breeder or local kennel club. Most instructors allow puppies as young as five months old to begin training classes.

At these classes, owners learn how to teach their dogs to stand squarely and still, or to stack, for the judge's examination. Using food tidbits such as liver, chicken, or string cheese will help keep the dog's attention and teach him to remain motionless.

Show dogs never sit in the show ring. They stand so the judge can have the best view of their bodies. If your dog has already been taught to sit, especially before receiving his food dish, begin teaching the "stand" command. If he begins to sit, quickly put a food treat near his mouth and lure him into a standing position. Pop the treat into his mouth when he's standing. Repeat this a few times and he'll soon realize that he only receives a treat when he stands.

At a conformation show, the judge performs an exam to determine how closely a dog conforms to the breed standard. The judge will look at the dog's overall outline, examine the teeth and ears, pick up the feet, and lift the tail. If the dog is a male, the judge will feel the testicles. Throughout the whole process, the dog must stand still.

Accustoming your dog to this level of handling—and from a stranger—will require a lot of practice. Each day at home, you should take your dog through the steps a

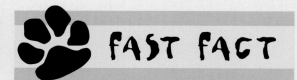

FAST FACT

In Junior Showmanship classes, which are open to children as young as eight, young people are judged on how well they handle their purebred dogs.

conformation judge would follow in performing a show examination.

LEAD TRAINING

At a show, dogs must gait, or trot, on the handler's left side without pulling on the leash. This allows the judge to see the dog's true structure as defined in the breed standard. In a show-ring gait, dog and handler must move in unison.

You can begin working on your dog's show-ring gait once he knows how to walk politely on a leash without pulling you. At a medium pace, trot with your dog in a straight line. If your dog pulls on the leash, stop suddenly and wait a few seconds before continuing. Your dog will soon realize that every time he strains at the leash the privilege of running is taken away.

Go about 30 to 40 feet in a straight line, then turn around and gait back. This maneuver is called the "down and back," and it is one of the

DOG SHOW CLASSES

With the exception of the Best of Breed category, males and females are shown separately in one of these classes. Ribbons are awarded for first through fourth place in each class of males and females. The first-place male from each class goes on to compete for Winners Dog. A runner-up, known as the Reserve Winner, is also chosen. The first-place female from each class competes for Winners Bitch. The Winners Dog and the Winners Bitch win the points and compete against other champions for Best of Breed.

Dog show entrants compete in the following classes:

Puppy: This class has two subdivisions—6 to 9 months, and 9 to 12 months.

12 to 18 Months: This is open to any dog that falls within the age range.

Novice: Dogs of any age are eligible for this class, as long as they have not won three first prizes in the Novice class; a first prize in a Bred by Exhibitor, American Bred, or Open class; or any points toward their championships.

Bred by Exhibitor: Dogs in this class must be owned and shown by their breeder.

American Bred: Only dogs bred and born in the United States are eligible to compete in this class.

Open: This class is for any dog that is at least six months of age.

Best of Breed: Eligible dogs are those that have already won a championship title, plus the Winners Dog and the Winners Bitch.

With patience and practice you can learn how to show your own dog. Pick up pointers by watching others at shows and attending classes.

primary ways a judge evaluates dogs in the ring. When the return trip ends, move in front of your dog and give him a small treat. If your dog pulls on the leash, stop suddenly and wait a few seconds, then continue.

To teach your up-and-coming star how to free-bait, or move his feet into the correct stacked position without you having to do it, give him a small food treat while maneuvering the leash until he stands correctly. This takes some time to practice, so be patient. You can pick up new techniques by going to dog shows without your dog and watching how other people handle their dogs in the ring. Tune in to televised dog shows to see the nuances of showing your breed.

Another great way to see how handlers show their dogs is to visit the Westminster Kennel Club's Web site (www.westminsterkennelclub.org).

PRACTICE SESSIONS

Effective training requires practice. With puppies, keep practice sessions very brief—three to five minutes at a time is usually sufficient. Adult dogs

EARNING CHAMPIONSHIP POINTS

To become a champion, a show dog must win 15 points, including two wins that are worth 3, 4, or 5 points (called "majors"). The majors must be won under two different judges. The AKC's Web site lists the point schedule for various shows.

Once dogs complete their championships, they can continue showing in the Best of Breed category and accumulate a national breed ranking. Dogs are ranked according to how many dogs in their breed they defeat. At this level dog showing is highly competitive and expensive, requiring extensive travel and a busy show schedule. To continue showing week after week, a dog must truly love to be the center of attention. There's no substitute for expert training and handling skills, which are necessary to keep the dog at the top of his game.

can handle 20-minute practices. Stack your dog up a few times, give a treat or two, and practice moving on the leash up and back and in a circle. Remember to keep it light and fun so the pup will look forward to practicing and doesn't become bored.

Once your dog has learned the basics, he's ready to enter some informal practice shows, called matches. No points are awarded at these shows, but they're a great way to rehearse for a regular show. Kennel clubs put on matches about once a year.

CHAPTER TEN

Volunteering for Service

While hanging out or playing catch with your dog is fun, there's another way to enjoy his company. Think good deeds. You and your dog can become a therapy team, helping people who could use some furry, four-footed love. Consider giving back to your community by lending a hand and a paw.

Most facilities that use therapy dog teams require membership in a pet therapy organization that screens its volunteers. Although every group has different health and training requirements, all dogs should pass the AKC's noncompetitive Canine Good Citizen test or have certification from the Delta Society Pet

Well-trained pets can help lift the spirits of sick or elderly people.

Partners Program (www.delta society.org) or Therapy Dogs International (www.tdi-dog.org).

CANINE GOOD CITIZEN

The Canine Good Citizen (CGC) program rewards dogs with good manners at home and in the community. Many people use the CGC program as a foundation for other performance activities, such as obedience and agility.

For CGC program certification, dogs must:

1. Accept a friendly stranger.
2. Sit politely for petting.
3. Be well groomed and not show any signs of aggression.
4. Walk on a loose leash.
5. Walk through a crowd without jumping, pulling, or acting fearful.
6. Sit and down on command and stay in place.
7. Come when called.
8. Show no more than a passing interest in another dog when approached by someone walking a dog.
9. Remain calm in an ordinary situation.
10. Remain well behaved when left alone for three minutes with another person.

DOG THERAPY

Dogs have an almost magical capacity to brighten the spirits of people who are isolated or ill. A visit from a therapy dog can work wonders in a hospital ward, nursing home, or mental-health facility. The dog brings a bit of lively entertainment and a welcome change from the routine. The psychological benefits include reduced feelings of loneliness, reduced stress, and a sense of emotional connection.

Therapy dog programs will accept purebred and mixed-breed dogs of all shapes and sizes, if the dogs are well trained. To prepare your dog, take him to a variety of public places so he becomes accustomed to strange sights and sounds. Reward him for greeting people politely, and socialize him around other dogs so

FAST FACT

Being around a dog, research shows, has physiological and psychological benefits for people. It lowers blood pressure, reduces anxiety, and can produce a general feeling of well-being. Patients who visit with animals are more likely to recover after a heart attack, and they are less troubled by minor complaints such as headache, backache, and flu.

he learns to show little interest in them when you're on duty.

Therapy dogs must be confident and steady. When it comes to entertaining patients, it's a bonus if your dog doesn't mind wearing a costume either. People love to see cute dogs in bunny ears at Easter; red, white, and blue Uncle Sam suits for the Fourth of July; Batman wings during Halloween; or reindeer antlers at Christmas.

If your dog can shake hands, nose a patient's hand, and give kisses, he will be a popular visitor. To teach your dog how to shake hands, support the paw without squeezing it. Avoid grabbing the foot or holding it too long. Lift the paw from behind and offer your other hand in front for your dog to shake.

Patients love receiving dog kisses. But you should stop your dog by gently pulling his head back with your hand if he gets carried away with the love-fest. Another, less intrusive way your dog can greet a patient is by nosing the patient's hand. Most dogs do this naturally. But to prepare your dog to use his snout in a good way, start by placing a few treats in your hand. Tell your dog "find it" when he begins to nose your hand, then release the treat. This is the cue you can use when you go visiting, but your dog should nose a patient's hand without the treat.

Small dogs make great bed snugglers. Dogs that are too big to greet a patient on a bed or to sit on a lap should master the command "stand for petting." Use food treats to teach this command. Lure the dog into a standing position by putting the goody in the flat of your hand toward the dog and pulling the goody from

THE RIGHT STUFF

Good volunteer dogs should be:

- Well behaved, friendly, and outgoing.
- Confident, relaxed, and unfazed by unusual noises.
- Willing to lie or sit quietly beside a patient.
- Comfortable wearing an identifying jacket or bandana.
- Well groomed, clean, and odor-free, with short nails.
- Tolerant of petting.

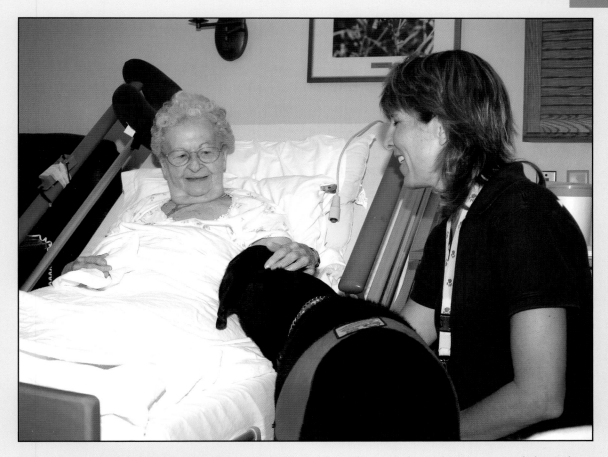

Dogs that have a calm, even temperament and a love for people make great candidates for therapy work.

his nose to a few inches away. He should automatically stand in an attempt to eat the treat. When he does, give him the food and say, "Good stand!"

PET THERAPY VISITATIONS

Before visiting with patients, exercise and play with your dog for a short time. Make sure he has used the potty, but also pack a plastic bag you can use in the event of an acci-

dent. Be sure to keep your dog on a short four-foot leash to prevent him from wandering the hallways. Don't let your dog sniff any medical supplies or a patient's open wound.

Always ask patients if they want to touch, pet, or hold your dog. While you may want to encourage the contact, if a patient says no, respect that decision. If you have a small dog, present him at the patient's waist or below, not near face level. Protect your dog from getting poked in his face by presenting him sideways or backwards.

If the patient wants to hold your dog, avoid handing the dog over in the patient's arms or hands. You can't be sure how steady the patient is, and you wouldn't want your dog to fall. Instead, place your dog in the patient's lap.

Always remain with your dog while visiting a patient. This is for your dog's safety and because the patient needs both of you as a visiting team.

PET-ASSISTED THERAPY

You and your dog can take service to another level through assisted therapy. This usually involves one dog-

People who are emotionally traumatized because of a serious illness or physical handicap may find comfort in the nonjudgmental affection of a dog. Therapy pets can help such patients open up to something outside themselves and begin to heal.

and-handler team assigned to one patient. The team works under the direction of a health care or human services professional such as an occupational, physical, or speech therapist. The assisted therapy is part of the patient's overall treatment program. The health care provider sets specific goals for the patient and consults with the handler on how the dog can help accomplish those goals through animal-assisted activities.

When a 16-year-old girl at a hospital in New Jersey was unable to use her hands and no therapy seemed to work, the staff brought in Cara, a black Standard Poodle. Giving Cara, a trained assistance

BE A PUPPY RAISER

If you have a loving home and would love to make a real difference to someone who is sight-impaired, consider training a guide dog. Many guide dog organizations need volunteer foster families to raise guide-puppies-in-training. Puppies go to foster families for age-appropriate socialization and obedience training around 8 to 12 weeks of age. All raisers attend regular training classes with the organization. Foster families provide a safe environment for a puppy and teach the puppy manners and basic commands.

While experience is usually not required, puppy raisers must be available throughout the day to care for their four-footed charges. They must commit to taking pups on outings and socialize them to new sights, sounds, and experiences in the community. Caring for a foster pup is an excellent way to have fun while helping to provide the gift of sight for someone.

Hearing-dogs-in-training also need puppy raisers. Hearing dogs learn how to respond to sounds and alert their owners 24 hours a day. But, as with guide dogs, they need good socialization and basic training first. For someone who cannot hear warning alarms, having a hearing dog can mean the difference between life and death. A hearing dog twirls in circles when the smoke alarm goes off, scratches at the phone when it rings, and goes to the door when the mailman comes. When you raise a hearing puppy, you provide a solid foundation for him and the person he will help.

Other organizations that train service dogs for the wheelchair-bound need puppy raisers too. To locate organizations in your community, ask your veterinarian for referrals or contact the Canine Companions for Independence (www.cci.org).

Reading Assistance Education Dogs (READ) is a national program that has been credited with helping students who are struggling to learn how to read. Many teachers say that students who participate feel comfortable and excited about reading to their canine companions. The dogs listen attentively while students read at their own pace. This provides a less intimidating environment than reading to adults or other students.

dog, a food treat was the girl's therapy, and she kept trying until she could do it.

READING EDUCATION ASSISTANCE DOGS

If you enjoy reading and want to volunteer with your dog to help developmentally disabled children and adults improve their reading skills, consider joining the Reading Education Assistance Dogs (READ) program. Registered therapy dogs and their handlers go to schools, libraries, and other settings and act as literacy mentors.

As reading companions, dogs help increase relaxation. When children read to dogs they improve their reading skills, learn to enjoy reading more, and overcome apprehension about reading out loud. Unlike classmates, who can sometimes be mean, a dog never makes fun of poor readers for making a mistake.

Before getting started, your dog should visit the veterinarian for a checkup. Organizations screen dogs for skills, temperament, and manners before they can begin the program.

Your dog needs to be outgoing, friendly and confident, and willing to be held by a stranger for two minutes while you disappear. This demonstrates overall sociability. Dogs that are calm, passive around children, and well socialized should do well.

EDUCATION OUTREACH PRESENTATIONS

If you and your dog would enjoy visiting schools, retirement communi-

FAST FACT

Service dogs can be trained to help patients who depend on ventilators to breathe. The dogs can retrieve an air hose that has become disconnected.

ties, and other facilities, consider joining a pet outreach program. During visits, you can discuss and demonstrate topics such as pet safety, dog bite prevention, hot weather tips, how to choose the right dog, pet care and grooming, and dog manners.

Many kennel clubs and shelters organize pet visits to local facilities for trained dogs and their handlers. Dogs must be vaccinated, and most organizations require a screening process for teams.

CHAPTER ELEVEN

Games and Tricks

Like people, dogs need to have some fun. Use games and a bit of trick training to amuse your canine companion. These capers will have the additional benefit of increasing your dog's ability to pay attention.

FOOD PUZZLE TOYS

Food puzzle toys are designed to give your dog something mentally challenging to do while you're away. Inside these toys are small food treats, which the dog has to figure

Both you and your dog can derive entertainment through playing with bubbles.

out how to get. There's usually a hole in one end of the toy, and the dog has to shake, paw, roll, or lick the toy to coax out the food. In addition to a tasty treat, your dog will get a sense of satisfaction from solving the puzzle.

Food puzzle toys are available in most pet supply stores. Many healthy treats are made specially to fit into these toys. But you can also use cheese, small pieces of chicken, hot dogs, apples, pears, peas, zucchini, carrots, kibble, or biscuits.

FUN AND GAMES

Playing interactive games with your dog will not only give him a good physical and mental workout, but also build his problem-solving skills and reinforce his desire to come to you when called. Many interactive games are great to play indoors, when you're short on time or the weather is too nasty to take your dog outside.

HIDE-AND-SEEK: When playing canine hide-and-seek, your dog receives a reward for finding you. Nothing could be more fun than that. Before beginning, make sure you have a few tasty goodies or some of your dog's favorite toys. Tell him to sit and stay or lie down and stay. With your dog's treats in your hand

or pocket, walk into another room and find an easy hiding place.

Call your dog to come to you, but do it only once. Wait while he looks for you. As soon as he locates you, praise him and give him a treat or toss him his toy. If your dog has trouble hunting you down, then hide in a place where you're partially visible. As he grasps the concept and locates you, choose more difficult hiding spots.

ROUND-ROBIN: This is a rainy-day game the whole family can enjoy. With everyone spread out in one room, take turns calling your dog and praising him or giving him a food treat when he comes. To help your dog focus on the next person calling him, the last person to call him should look away and put hands and treats behind his or her back. Once your dog gets the hang of this game, spread out into different parts of the house where you can't see each other. As before, take turns calling the dog. If the weather is nice, take the game outside.

WATER AND BUBBLE PLAY: Using water to engage your dog in safe, outdoor fun also provides great exercise. Use a hose sprayer attachment to entice your dog to chase a stream of water a few feet away from him.

Many dogs love to run after the water and try to bite it.

Bubbles are another popular source of outdoor high jinks. Special doggy toys produce odd-shaped bubbles with a chicken, peanut butter, or bacon flavor that dogs can't resist.

TRICKS

There's a trick to teaching your dog tricks. You have to break the trick down into small parts that your dog can learn in sequence. These lead up to the whole caper. Be patient and give out plenty of your dog's favorite treats to maintain his motivation.

SHAKE PAWS: Dogs that are very willing to please you will learn this in a flash. For dogs that like to test their dominance, this might take a while. Eventually, however, your dog will come around.

To teach your dog how to shake his paw, have some food treats nearby. With your dog sitting in front of

Most dogs can learn to "shake" fairly quickly.

NO FREEBIES

Many new dog owners hand out food treats anytime their dog looks cute or wags his tail. Resist this temptation. Instead, ask your dog to work for his goody. This will help him exercise his brain, and he'll become more compliant. When you take your dog for a walk, tell him to sit before you open the door. After he does what you ask, hand him a food tidbit. Ask him to sit down before beginning a game of tug-of-war. Use game times and tricks as training opportunities, and reserve the treats for those special times.

you at your eye level, pick up one his paws and tickle the back of it. When he lifts that paw, praise him by saying, "good shake" and give him a treat.

You may need to repeat this several times before your dog begins to lift his paw without your having to tickle it. Next ask him to "shake," and reach for the paw. When he lifts it by himself, praise him and give him a food treat.

Increase the difficulty slightly by holding your palm at his mid-chest level. Ask him to "shake." Hopefully he'll plop his paw into your raised palm. To teach him to shake the other paw, tickle the back of that paw and repeat the instructions but say, "Other paw!"

HIGH FIVE: This builds on the shake paws trick. Extend your palm at your dog's mid-chest level and say, "shake." As he reaches, move your palm to his chin level. Praise and reward him when he touches your palm. Repeat the process, raising your palm a few inches higher each time, until your dog stretches his paw as high as he can.

PLAY DEAD: Children love to see a dog pull off this stunt. Tell your dog to lie down. Lean over him and say, "bang" as you point your index finger

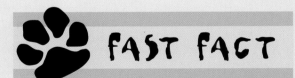

FAST FACT

A good game of fetch teaches your dog how to drop items when you ask for them. To teach your dog to fetch, show him a toy and toss it a short distance away. When he picks it up and returns to you, say, "give" or "drop it" and give him a treat.

at him. If he rolls over on his side or back, reward him with the treat. If he doesn't roll over, use the treat to lure him into that position. Then praise him. You'll need to repeat this a few times until he responds to your "bang" command.

Once he masters this, call him to you from a standing position and say, "bang." If he follows the command and lies down, give him a treat. If not, you may need to physically place him in this position a few

times. Add difficulty by increasing your dog's distance from you to two or four feet.

JUMP THROUGH ARMS: If you have a small dog, this is a great caper. People love to see a little dog flying through the air. Start by using a hula hoop, and keep your dog on a leash. With the bottom edge of the hoop resting on the ground, let your dog sniff the hoop. Draw the leash through the hoop and use a treat to

Amuse your friends by teaching your dog to jump through your arms.

lure your dog through it while saying, "jump." When he walks through to eat the treat, praise him.

Repeat the process, this time with the hoop a few inches off the ground. Each time you do the exercise, raise the hoop a little higher, until the bottom is at your dog's eye level. He'll have to jump to get through the hoop.

Now your dog is ready to perform the trick without his leash. Say, "jump," then praise him lavishly when he leaps through the hoop. Add more difficulty by slowly pivoting in a circle with the hoop when you ask him to jump. Finally, substitute your arms in a circle for the hoop.

BALANCING A TREAT: This may look cruel, but it tests your dog's willingness to please you by balancing the treat first and gobbling it later. To begin, tell your dog to sit in front of you. Reward him with a click or a treat, or by telling him he's a good dog for sitting. Next, hold your dog's muzzle beneath the chin and place a small food treat on his nose. If you have a flat-faced breed there's a nice little space between his eyes that will hold a treat nicely.

Slowly release your dog's chin and tell him, "stay." If he holds it for a brief moment, say, "OK, good boy,"

FAST FACT

Wrestling and roughhousing with your dog is not a good idea. These activities will only teach him to bite and to use his strength against people rather than to cooperate.

and click. This gives him permission to drop his head and eat the treat. Gradually increase the time your dog holds the treat on his nose.

WANT TO APOLOGIZE?: This begins with you asking your dog if he regrets any recent poor decisions, then the word "Apologize." With your dog facing you, instruct him, "down." When he puts his head down, say "apologize," and click or draw your hand holding a treat down to the ground. As soon as his head touches the ground, give him the treat at ground level. Repeat by lengthening the time your dog keeps his head on the ground. Each time, repeat the word "apologize" to remind your dog to lie down and lower his head to the ground. Be sure to reward him with a treat when he holds the position for 10 to 20 seconds.

CLEAN UP YOUR TOYS: This is an impressive trick that never fails to

Teaching your dog to apologize can be challenging, but with enough practice and treats, he'll eventually understand what you want.

amuse guests. Plus, this practical prank will help you out before you need to vacuum. Keep a toy box handy for the collection. Give your dog a toy and tell him, "take it." When your dog has the toy in his mouth, click and give him a treat to reward him for first holding it, then releasing it for the food.

Next, place the toy box between your feet and tell your dog, "come."

Repeat the process above, so that he takes the toy in his mouth and holds it over the top of the box. Tell your dog, "leave it," and click. When he drops the toy into the box, give him the treat.

Once he's mastered this aspect of the trick, follow up by placing the toy on the floor a distance away from the box and telling him, "take it." When he does, reward him for picking up the toy, and encourage him to leave it in the box. Once your dog follows these directions consistently, you can replace the commands with a new instruction, "clean up toys."

FETCH THIS BOOK

Asking your dog to fetch an object and return it to you is always a fun trick. Your dog can go after just about anything you train him to retrieve, such as this book, his leash, a dog bowl, or your cell phone. Just be careful that his teeth don't dial long distance as he is carrying the phone to you!

To teach your dog how to fetch this book, he needs to learn to find it, pick it up, and deliver it to you. Here's where a clicker comes in handy. Begin by handing your dog the book and click. When he takes the book from you, click and quickly give him a treat. To take the treat he'll open his mouth to release the book, so be ready to catch it. Repeat this a few more times.

Next, put the book in another area of the room, letting him see where it is. Tell your dog, "go get the book." Click and treat him when he picks it up in his mouth and gives it to you.

Your dog will master this after a few training sessions. Now, you can put the book in another room where he can easily find it, and tell your

dog, "go get the book." He may be a little tentative at first, so you may have to walk into the room with him and show him what you want.

Once your dog has got the hang of the trick, you can start making it a bit more challenging to find the book—or whatever object you want him to bring you. If you want your dog to fetch different things, use a different command phrase (for example, "go get the leash") for each item. Always remember, too, that this is meant to be an enjoyable game for your dog. Don't get frustrated if it takes her a while to learn—have fun with training.

Dog training is rewarding for everyone involved.

Organizations to Contact

American Kennel Club
260 Madison Ave.
New York, NY 10016
Phone: 212-696-8200
E-mail: info@akc.org
Web site: www.akc.org

Association of Pet Dog Trainers
150 Executive Center Dr., Box 35
Greenville, SC 29615
Phone: 800-738-3647
Fax: 864-331-0767
E-mail: information@apdt.com
Web site: www.apdt.com

Canadian Kennel Club
200 Ronson Dr., Suite 400
Etobicoke, Ontario
M9W 5Z9 Canada
Phone: 416-675-5511
Fax: 416-675-6506
E-mail: information@ckc.ca
Web site: www.ckc.ca/en

**Canine Companions
for Independence**
PO Box 446
Santa Rosa, CA 95402-0446
Phone: 866-224-3647
Web site: www.cci.org

Delta Society
875 124th Avenue NE, Suite 101
Bellevue, WA 98005
Phone: 425-226-7357
Fax: 425-679-5539
Web site: www.deltasociety.org

**International Association of
Canine Professionals**
PO Box 560156
Montverde, FL 34756-0156
Phone: 407-469-2008
E-mail: iacpadmin@mindspring.com
Web site: www.canineprofessionals.com

The Kennel Club of the U.K.
1-5 Clarges Street
London W1J 8AB
United Kingdom
Phone: 0870 606 6750
Fax: 020 7518 1058
Web site: www.thekennelclub.org.uk

**National Association of Dog
Obedience Instructors**
PMB 369
729 Grapevine Highway
Hurst, TX 76054-2085
E-mail: corrsec2@nadoi.org
Web site: www.nadoi.org

**National Association
for Search and Rescue**
Educator Course/Exam Packets
PO Box 232020
Centreville, VA 20120-2020
Phone: 703-222-6277
E-mail: info@nasar.org
Web site: www.nasar.org

**North American Dog Agility
Council (NADAC)**
11522 South Highway 3
Cataldo, ID 83810
E-mail: info@nadac.com
Web site: www.nadac.com

**North American Flyball
Association (NAFA)**
1400 West Devon Avenue, #512
Chicago, IL 60660
Phone and fax: 800-318-6312
E-mail: flyball@flyball.org
Web site: www.flyball.org

Splash Dogs
640 Bailey Rd., Suite 400
Pittsburg, CA 94565
Phone: 925-793-619
Fax: 925-226-4655
E-mail: Tony@splashdogs.com
Web site: www.splashdogs.com

Therapy Dogs International, Inc.
88 Bartley Road
Flanders, NJ 07836
Phone: 973-252-9800
Fax: 973-252-7171
E-mail: tdi@gti.net
Web site: www.tdi-dog.org

United Kennel Club
100 E. Kilgore Rd.
Kalamazoo, MI 49002-5584
Phone: 269-343-9020
Fax: 269-343-7037
Web site: www.ukcdogs.com

**United States Dog Agility
Association, Inc. (USDAA)**
P.O. Box 850955
Richardson, TX 75085-0955
Phone: 972-487-2200
Fax: 972-272-4404
E-mail: info@usdaa.com
Website: www.usdaa.com

**World Canine Freestyle
Organization (WCFO)**
P.O. Box 350122
Brooklyn, NY 11235-2525
Phone: 718-332-8336
Fax: 718-646-2686
E-mail: wcfodogs@aol.com
Web site: www.worldcanine
freestyle.org

Time spent training will help build a strong bond between you and your dog.

Further Reading

Bridwell, Jennifer. *The Everything Dog Obedience Book*. Avon, Mass.: Adams Media, 2007.

Clothier, Suzanne. *Bones Would Rain from the Sky: Deepening Our Relationships With Dogs*. New York: Grand Central Publishing, 2005.

Fogle, Dr. Bruce. *New Dog*. New York: Firefly Books, 2008.

Killion, Jane. *When Pigs Fly—Training Success with Impossible Dogs*. Wenatchee, Wash.: Dogwise Publishing, 2007.

McConnell, Patricia. *For the Love of a Dog: Understanding Emotion in You and Your Best Friend*. New York: Ballantine Books, 2007.

Miller, Pat. *The Power of Positive Dog Training*. Hoboken, N.J.: Wiley Publishing, Inc., 2008.

Rugaas, Turid. *On Talking Terms with Dogs: Calming Signals*. 2nd edition. Wenatchee, Wash.: Dogwise Publishing, 2005.

Schade, Victoria. *Bonding with Your Dog*. Hoboken, N.J.: Wiley Publishing, Inc. 2009.

Silverman, Joel. *What Color Is Your Dog?* Freehold, N.J.: Kennel Club Books, 2009.

Sundance, Kyra. *The Dog Rules*. New York: Fireside, 2009.

Internet Resources

http://www.aspca.org

> The ASPCA's Web site offers tips on adoption, pet care, and behavior as well as information on animal legislation, service animal policies, pet overpopulation, and dangerous dogs.

http://www.clickertraining.com

> Everything you need to know about training your dog using a clicker, hosted by expert Karen Pryor.

http://dogchannel.com

> Hosted by Bowtie Inc., this Web site includes articles published in Dog Fancy and Dog World magazines.

http://www.hsus.org

> The Humane Society of the United States hosts a comprehensive Web site about all aspects of dog care.

http://www.patriciamcconnell.com

> A great source of training information from Patricia McConnell, a renowned training expert.

http://www.thedogdaily.com

Here's a comprehensive Web site written by top experts covering all aspects of dog care.

http://www.veterinarypartner.com

This Web site provides up-to-date animal health information and general information about a variety of canine topics, including behavior and training.

Index

Numbers in **bold italics** refer to captions.

Contributors

A dog owner and trainer all her life, **ELAINE WALDORF GEWIRTZ** writes about human and canine behavior, care, health, and training. The author of books and articles, Elaine is a multiple recipient of the prestigious Maxwell Award from the Dog Writers' Association of America. Her writing has also garnered the ASPCA Humane Issues Award and the Wiley/Ellsworth S. Howell Award.

Senior Consulting Editor **GARY KORSGAARD, DVM,** has had a long and distinguished career in veterinary medicine. After graduating from The Ohio State University's College of Veterinary Medicine in 1963, he spent two years as a captain in the Veterinary Corps of the U.S. Army. During that time he attended the Walter Reed Army Institute of Research and became Chief of the Veterinary Division for the Sixth Army Medical Laboratory at the Presidio, San Francisco.

In 1968 Dr. Korsgaard founded the Monte Vista Veterinary Hospital in Concord, California, where he practiced for 32 years as a small animal veterinarian. He is a past president of the Contra Costa Veterinary Association, and was one of the founding members of the Contra Costa Veterinary Emergency Clinic, serving as president and board member of that hospital for nearly 30 years.

Dr. Korsgaard retired in 2000. He enjoys golf, hiking, international travel, and spending time with his wife Susan and their three children and four grandchildren.